# *Partnering*
# in Action

*A guide for building successful collaboration*
*across organizational boundaries*

Diane K. Fasel

**PATHWAYS**

First published in 2000 by
How To Books Ltd, 3 Newtec Place,
Magdalen Road, Oxford OX4 1RE, United Kingdom
Tel: 01865 793806   Fax: 01865 248780

British Library Cataloguing in Publication Data
A catalogue record for this book is available from
the British Library

Edited by Diana Brueton   Cover image PhotoDisc
Cover design by Shireen Nathoo Design

Produced for How To Books by Deer Park Productions
Typeset by Anneset, Weston-super-Mare, Somerset
Printed and bound in Great Britain
by The Cromwell Press Ltd., Trowbridge, Wiltshire

Note: The material contained in this book is set out in good
faith for general guidance and no liability can be accepted for loss or expense
incurred as a result of relying in particular circumstances on statements made in
the book. Laws and regulations are complex and liable to change, and readers
should check the current position with the relevant authorities before making
personal arrangements.

*Pathways is an imprint of*
How To Books

# Contents

# List of Illustrations

Dedication

With gratitude and affection to my clients, associates, friends and family who have taught me *Partnering in Action.*

# Preface

This book is intended to stimulate your thinking and motivate you to create and sustain successful business partnering relationships. It is about the ongoing process of building collaboration across organizational boundaries. As with any relationship, if you take collaboration for granted, you lose it; if you nurture collaboration, it thrives.

This book contains a potpourri of concepts and ideas, along with vignettes from real-world situations – all organized around six keys to collaboration:

> Part 1 describes a methodology – *Partnering in Action* – that you can use to build successful partnering relationships.
>
> Part 2 offers some notes on how to get started and how to sustain *Partnering in Action.*

This book is based on many years of learning – observation, practice, success. Its contents are based on proven management practice, demonstrated leadership skill, models for interpersonal behavior, and good old common sense.

Also, this book represents *Partnering in Action.* A special thanks to Giles Lewis, Nikki Read and Rosalind Loten of How To Books for their guidance throughout the publishing process; Emily Nadeau of Words, Ink, for assembling all the pieces; Abe Darwish for his kind introduction and faithful application of *Partnering in Action* methodology; and Bill Stockton for his ongoing encouragement and support.

This writing will represent time well spent if it serves to:

- Refresh your memory so that you apply the good things you already know.
- Reframe concepts and ideas for you so that you can apply them in a new way.
- Rekindle your enthusiasm for making a personal difference in your collaborative relationships.

With all best wishes, may you enjoy successful collaboration across organizational boundaries.

*Diane K. Fasel*

*These partnering concepts can be applied to all functions in all industries.*

# Foreword

M y interest in business partnering began many years ago out of my fascination with negotiation and many opportunities to negotiate deals with others as part of my work. Guidance given to me early on was that I get 'the best deal possible'. What I found out through experience is that 'the best deal possible' has to be win-win. So I began to look for relationships instead of deals – partnering relationships. I didn't use the word 'partnering' at the beginning, but the concepts were the same – collaborative business relationships that are built and sustained on mutual trust and respect, aligned around common objectives, committed to mutual success, and grown based on continuous learning.

I have found that these partnering concepts are universal. They can be applied to all functions and all industries. Allowing for cultural differences, the concepts of partnering can be applied worldwide across all kinds of organizational boundaries.

Today, I manage the worldwide real estate and site services organization as a vice president for 3Com Corporation. This worldwide team uses partnering concepts in all aspects of its work, ranging from discrete projects to daily sustaining operations activities. We have included in our partnering efforts both other 3Com employees from around the world as well as many different outside vendors, suppliers, consultants, architects and contractors:

◆ We have designed and constructed six major campus sites around the world, totaling more than 3.1 million square feet. These campuses include office space, manufacturing floor, engineering laboratories and site amenities. Many of these projects have involved demanding scope of requirements, short timeframes and tight budgets. Partnering has helped us to achieve better business results with a sense of personal satisfaction.

◆ Our internal customers' business objectives drive the real estate and site services team's priorities. We have had to deal with changes in the company's business direction, fast and slow business growth, mergers, acquisitions, spin-offs, and organizational restructuring. Because of these dynamics, our site services sustaining operations are anything but static. That's where partnering has helped us. Through strategic partnering relationships we maintain a flexible and scalable organization. Food service, security and safety functions, building maintenance and operations, space management, and employee services all involve business partnering relationships with key outside suppliers, vendors and consultants. We have to keep business partnering relationships collaborative and healthy in order to anticipate changes that will affect the business, and to respond quickly and effectively to customers' changing needs.

As we continue in this new millennium the demands of business and the need for organizations to be agile and scalable will accelerate. Globalization of businesses – shrinking time to market requirements for new products and services – fierce competition everywhere; all of these ingredients offer a context for why partnering will become even more of a critical success factor for businesses.

My colleagues and I have benefited in many ways from Diane Fasel's work. Through her approach to *Partnering in Action* and her personal facilitation skills, she has helped us focus on the process of partnering, specifically to:

- ◆ Understand the business context first, as background for any partnering relationship.
- ◆ Clarify objectives, priorities, roles and responsibilities for our projects as well as our sustaining operations responsibilities.
- ◆ Ensure alignment among all parties, both employees and outside partner organizations and individuals.
- ◆ Match skills and interests of individuals and organizations with business needs, project requirements and sustaining operations responsibilities.
- ◆ Look for partnering behavior characteristics in others in addition to technical or functional expertise.
- ◆ Be more explicit about mutual trust and respect among team members.

- Improve our interpersonal skills so that we can accomplish more together with less effort.
- Benefit from what we learn, both good and bad, by incorporating lessons learned into future activities.
- Pay attention to both the tasks at hand and the partnering relationship itself, knowing that true partnering requires both successful achievement of tasks and enduring relationships.

On a personal note, through this process I have changed as a leader. I have had to become more of a role model for good partnering. For example, in situations where I might have removed individuals or organizations from a team in the past, I have taken time to check for alignment and guide or coach them in new ways. In addition, I have learned to become more of a conductor rather than a taskmaster. Through partnering I have grown to appreciate and value the diversity of a workforce that includes both internal employees and outside partners worldwide, different work styles and many points of view. And, I am still evolving.

As you read this book I encourage you to reflect on your own business partnering experiences – notice what has worked well for you and what has not. Then, identify some of the ideas presented here that you can apply now. I believe you will find that they make a positive difference in your ability to develop successful collaboration across organizational boundaries. Good luck.

*Abe Darwish*
*Vice President*
*3Com Corporation*

# Introduction:
# The Case for *Partnering in Action*

G lobal marketplace – fierce competition – limited product life cycles – labor shortage – the need to respond quickly to business change. All are reasons that partnering with others is becoming more important.

> In order to thrive or even survive in today's business environment most organizations are finding that collaboration across organizational boundaries is necessary.

No longer can individuals, departments, functions, organizations, or even companies work in vacuums. For example:

- ◆ To get product to market quickly, a high tech start-up company relies on a network of independent distribution organizations. They go beyond the 'letter of the law' to create collaborative working relationships that capitalize on the strengths of each organization. They share information, make joint calls on prospects, solicit input from each other in order to build their respective businesses.
- ◆ To remain viable in the marketplace, the merger of two financial institutions requires speedy integration of two unique business entities. They develop a shared vision for their future together that:
  - builds on common values
  - utilizes 'best practices' from both institutions
  - treats customers with respect
  - manages transition carefully and thoughtfully for all involved
  - blends two distinct organizational cultures into one.
- ◆ To effect major change in a local community, elected officials on school board, city council, and hospital board work together across party and organizational boundaries. They set

aside their partisan agendas in order to:
- participate in dialogue with each other and with community members
- define a vision for their desired change
- create new cross-organizational entities to make the vision a reality
- develop an integrated process for including diverse individuals and organizations.

◆ To fund new technology development, major competitors join together in a strategic alliance. Together they create a new enterprise with a specific shared purpose while preserving intellectual capital for those organizations that participate in the venture. They:
- define protocol for how individuals are placed 'on assignment'
- develop 'rules of engagement' for operation within the venture
- determine how their success will be measured.

◆ To overcome product reliability problems in the marketplace, sales, product development and customer service organizations break down their operational barriers and work together. They create a cross-organizational team whose job it is to remove organizational obstacles and get results fast.

◆ Because of labor shortage in key skills, a service organization relies on contractors, consultants and temporary employees in ongoing partnering relationships. At the core of these relationships are:
- shared values
- clear purpose
- defined processes for getting their work done
- mutual trust and respect
- individuals who get the job done.

◆ Passionate about an idea for a new kind of company, executives in an engineering company, financial organization, manufacturers' representatives, along with several independent consultants and contractors, bring a new product to market. All involved have a common objective; they understand how to go about their work together; they rely on regular open and honest communication; and enjoy a high degree of trust and confidence in each other.

- To respond to customers' needs for different kinds of training services, an emerging company allies with many independent training providers to create and deliver the right solutions. This group looks for both individuals and organizations to partner with who share:
  - common customer satisfaction goals
  - core values that include collaboration and team work
  - commitment to strive for excellence in getting the job done
  - positive reputation in the marketplace.
- Committed to their long-standing partnering relationship, a team of owners' representatives, construction contractors, architects and consultants deliver a new building of world-class quality, cost-effectively and in record time. To accomplish this fast-paced project with changing customer requirements and time and budget constraints, the group:
  - checks for alignment of purpose and priorities on a regular basis through core team meetings and one-on-one conversations
  - relies on past performance and reputation to build confidence and trust among all involved
  - monitors progress and resolves problems and conflicts quickly, leaving nothing to fester for too long
  - captures lessons learned along the way.  ·
- In response to market changes, three independent entrepreneurial companies are purchased and merged into one. They must:
  - give up their separateness in favor of becoming one organization
  - get acquainted with each others' businesses – products and services and commitments to customers; operational processes and systems; people and organizational structures
  - determine together how they will move forward.
- To design and build a customized sailboat, a designer, builder, consultants, subcontractors and owner work together as a team. They:
  - develop a shared vision of the final product, and common expectations for how success will be measured
  - trust their colleagues to do the right job

- establish open and honest communication, and a process for designing and building which encourages creativity and innovation.

All of the above examples require collaboration across organizational boundaries. Some of these examples are internal to one enterprise. Others describe collaboration among individuals and/or across corporate boundaries.

These stories describe people making choices. Choices about:

♦ The kinds of relationships they create.
♦ Scope and duration of the ventures.
♦ Underlying purpose and measures of success.
♦ Whether and how individuals agree to work with each other.

How effective these business relationships are depends on the collaboration skills of all participants – to what degree they connect, coordinate and cooperate with each other.

The above stories and other stories like them disclose the basic nature of collaboration:

♦ The experience of collaborating with others across organizational boundaries can be good or bad depending on who is doing it and how it is being done.
♦ In some circumstances it is easy to work across organizational boundaries, and in others it is difficult.
♦ When done well, the experience of collaborating across organizational boundaries can be very rewarding.
♦ Some collaborative relationships are short-lived, while others are enduring.
♦ Collaboration is multi-faceted.
♦ There are many ways to achieve successful collaboration.
♦ To make collaboration work across boundaries requires explicit investment of time and energy of those involved.
♦ Demand for collaboration in business is increasing.

What the above stories have in common is they all are about people trying to achieve real business results in a dynamic, rapidly changing marketplace. Through effective collaboration these people and others like them create a balance of:

♦ high performance

- cost effectiveness
- personal satisfaction.

How about you? What is your business situation? Are you trying to:

- enable a corporate merger or acquisition
- create a joint venture or strategic alliance
- manage multiple companies or organizations for a fast-track development project
- outsource a function or service, with expectations of improved quality, enhanced flexibility or reduced cost
- create a sustaining business relationship with a key vendor or supplier
- become a better team mate personally?

If you answered yes to any of the above, then you are faced with a need to get people to work together effectively and efficiently. You must develop and maintain successful collaboration across organizational boundaries.

Whatever your circumstance, please know that you have a choice regarding how your experience will be. You can go along for the ride, at the mercy of whatever is going on around you, or you can navigate your own path with your colleagues and even guide them to have a favorable experience in working with you.

Depending on your level of skill and interest in collaboration, you can achieve bottom-line business results and have an enjoyable journey as well.

Part 1

# Methodology for Successful Collaboration

CHAPTER 1

# Methodology Overview

P artnering in Action is a management approach for creating and sustaining successful collaboration across organizational boundaries.

- ◆ Collaboration – the act of working together.
- ◆ Organizational boundaries – real or perceived barriers between individuals, work teams, groups, functions, departments, divisions, business units, corporations, associations, business enterprises.

## Choosing to Use *Partnering in Action*

*Partnering in Action* is a methodology that can be used by two or more individuals and/or organizations to achieve specific business objectives for single projects and long-term ventures. By using this methodology to develop and maintain real collaboration, you get a better result. You actually can achieve a balance of:

- ◆ high performance – accomplish your business result
- ◆ cost-effectiveness – use resources wisely
- ◆ personal satisfaction – enjoy the experience.

*Partnering in Action* is relevant for all kinds of enterprises in all industries. Allowing for cultural differences, this methodology offers benefits to:

- ◆ Internal collaboration. Individuals, work groups, departments, and divisions within the same organizational or corporate structure that need to work together to accomplish the enterprise's objectives.
- ◆ External collaboration. Independent consultants, contractors, companies and other enterprises that want to work together.
- ◆ Combinations. Internal and external individuals and entities that want to work together.

You can apply this methodology regardless of whether the individuals, organizations or business circumstances are old or new, large or small, global or local, for profit or not for profit.

This methodology can help you to:

- Select appropriate partners for a new cross-organizational collaborative venture.
- Start and provide ongoing guidance for a cross-organizational collaborative venture.
- Turn around a cross-organizational collaborative venture that is faltering.

*Partnering in Action* is not a ritual. It is not an excuse to go offsite and have a meeting where you and your colleagues can 'hang out' for a day or two.

> *Partnering in Action* is a 'way of life' for your collaboration – a choice, much like diet, exercise and religion.

You and your colleagues must choose with every interaction whether to be in a healthy, productive collaborative relationship or not.

To employ this methodology, you must align and integrate the why, what, how, and who of your business relationship. You:

- draw on individual and organizational strengths.
- maximize the effectiveness of each organization's resources.

## The Six Keys to *Partnering in Action*

As depicted in Figure 1 there are six keys to Partnering in Action. All six keys must be present to some degree, and they are interrelated, affecting each other. As you make changes in any one of the six areas, you impact your overall situation.

At both an individual and organizational level, *Partnering in Action* requires:

- **Alignment** – the arrangement or order of your venture that allows all pieces to fit together.
- **Ability** – the capacity of both individuals and organizations to act.
- **Attention** – regard for and vigilance about things that make collaboration work for your venture.

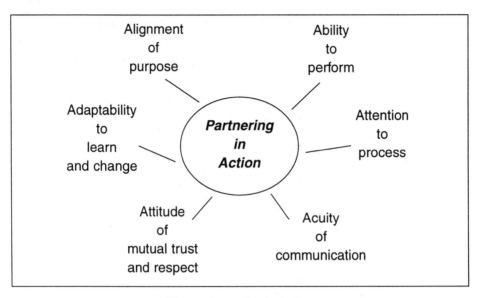

Fig. 1.   Partnering in Action.

- ◆ **Acuity** – keenness or sharpness of focus with respect to your collaboration.
- ◆ **Attitude** – the point of view or state of mind held by the individuals and organizations involved in your venture.
- ◆ **Adaptability** – flexibility and versatility on the parts of all involved to adjust their plans and activities as circumstances change.

At the same time *Partnering in Action* requires:
- ◆ **Purpose** – clear reason for your venture to exist, at this time, in this way.
- ◆ **Performance** – execution or accomplishment of real work by both individuals and organizations in your venture.
- ◆ **Processes** – the systematic series of actions taken by those involved in the collaboration in order to achieve the end result.
- ◆ **Communication** – the ongoing interchange among participants of thoughts, ideas, impressions, opinions, data, and information by speech, writing, or signs.
- ◆ **Trust and respect** – reliance by all of you on integrity, strength, and/or surety of others involved in the venture, and esteem or regard for them as members of the group.
- ◆ **Learning and change** – your ongoing transition as individuals

and organizations, becoming different from how you were as a result of participation in this venture.

It is hard to say whether any one of the six keys is more important than the others. To achieve successful collaboration across organizational boundaries, you need them all.

> The degree to which all six keys exist in harmony at the same time influences the degree to which you and your colleagues will achieve real collaboration.

Different people, in different business situations at different times, find different aspects of the partnering relationship more relevant. By focusing on any one of the six keys, you make progress in your chosen area of interest and impact all the others as well. For example:

- Some choose to focus on attitude of mutual trust and respect as the base on which to build their successful collaborative business relationship. They prefer to approach their business dealings from the basis of solid personal relationships. These collaborators spend time defining what it means to trust and respect their colleagues. They cite examples of where they experienced trusting relationships, and where trust was broken. They spend time just getting acquainted with their colleagues, finding out as much as they can about each other as people.
- Others prefer to concentrate on perfecting the processes for their venture, and on ensuring that everyone knows what he/she is supposed to do as a way to get clarity and define a positive, successful relationship. These collaborators count on clarity of role and responsibility and defined ways of doing things to provide the basis for working together. They determine in as much detail as possible, for every individual and organization, who will do what and how things will be done. They clarify authority levels, and protocol for decision-making and problem resolution. They develop and deploy systems, both manual and computer-based, to help them through the course of the venture.
- Still others prefer to concentrate on making sure all are aligned

regarding purpose for the venture. They define vision, values and high-level measures of success. They take time to ensure that all understand and buy into an overall goal. They trust that if the big picture is clear for all involved, the details will be easier to work out.

◆ Some need to concentrate on clarifying communication for their venture in order to build collaboration. They work together to determine what protocol they will use for meetings, conference calls, email messages and distribution of documents, as well as to agree on timeframes for response.

◆ Some prefer to look at their collaborative venture from the point of view of offering for all involved a learning opportunity right from the start. They determine at the onset of the venture how each participant will have to change to collaborate successfully in this specific situation.

All approaches work fine. The key is for you to work with your colleagues where they are – to build your collaborative relationship from the unique strengths and interests of those involved in your cross-organizational collaborative venture.

For example, suppose you take time up front to define the key processes to be used in your venture for decision making, problem resolution, progress reporting and so on. By doing so, you help to:

◆ streamline communication
◆ develop trust and respect among participants
◆ aid participants in doing their jobs.

Likewise, if you spend time developing trust and respect among participants, you automatically:

◆ improve communication
◆ strengthen both desire and ability of individuals to perform.

Where you focus attention first is largely a matter of personal choice and convenience. Every cross-organizational collaborative venture is unique. Therefore you and your colleagues must determine where the opportunities are.

If you are questioning where to begin to secure a successful business partnering relationship across organizational boundaries, begin with **alignment of purpose**. Experience shows that when there is a common purpose, other factors fall in place more easily. Once purpose is clear and all participants are in agreement, focus on any of the other five keys listed above.

Also, remember that to build collaboration people have to *want* to do so. *You cannot do this alone.* You must get your colleagues involved. Get others involved who have collaboration skills and interests. At the end of the day, if participants do not want to collaborate, nothing you can do will change that.

Even if you and your colleagues have worked together before, you must define and develop each specific relationship. This venture, in this business context, at this time.

> Don't assume that what worked for the last venture will apply even at all for this one.

By being conscious of your choices you have a much better chance of creating and sustaining a successful partnering relationship.

Individuals' backgrounds, experiences, skills, interests, expectations all make a difference. Organizations' customs, policies, operational processes, goals and objectives all impact your business relationship. Meanings and uses of words, measures of success, applications of rewards and recognition all represent opportunities for mismatch and/or mis-step. Your challenge is to navigate proactively in order to create success.

In a collaborative venture across organizational boundaries, you must bring the principals together early and often to manage success. In addition to whatever content expertise you bring to the venture, your ability to build and maintain relationships will serve you well. Moreover, your abilities to facilitate and coach others are critical – influencing them where they are.

At the core of *Partnering in Action* is *you* – how you behave, your thoughts, feelings, words, deeds. You choose whether to be a partner or not. You do this real time, interaction by interaction, as you go about your work.

Part One of this book provides helpful insights derived from real case studies regarding what it takes in a business venture to create and sustain collaboration across organizational boundaries:

◆ alignment of purpose
◆ ability to perform

- attention to process
- acuity of communication
- attitude of trust and respect
- adaptability to learn and change.

In addition, Part Two offers:
- some tips for getting started
- ideas for sustaining your collaboration
- the role of the leader(s)
- notes for you.

# CHAPTER 2

# Alignment of Purpose

*The more common the purpose, the more likely will be true collaboration.*

I n a collaborative venture you must establish clarity of purpose. One purpose, common to all involved. The more common the purpose, the more likely will be true collaboration.

An old adage states 'Stand for something or you will fall for anything'. Put another way, there is power in purpose. Like the bulls eye on a target for the archer or marksman, clarity of purpose provides something to aim for. Clarity of purpose transcends both individual and organizational biases, and serves as a fundamental unifying force for your collaborative venture. Clarity of purpose provides:

- meaning
- direction
- focus
- freedoms
- boundaries
- guidance.

To ensure a successful business partnering venture, you must pay attention to purpose. If you don't, it will exist as a hodge-podge of many individual purposes, potentially disjointed or conflicting. You and your colleagues represent these as your goals, objectives, intentions, expectations, hopes, dreams or desires. They encompass both philosophical concepts and pragmatic, results-oriented ideas. However represented, these purposes may be large or small, positive or negative, proactive or reactive, important or petty, well-articulated or fuzzy. And they are all present, to be reckoned with as part of your collaboration – a variety of different individual agendas, or worse yet a collection of 'hidden agendas'.

Just as there are many definitions for words or phrases, frequently there are as many perspectives and possibilities regarding purpose as there are people involved in the collaboration.

> You may think that you know the intentions and expectations
> of others, but unless you bring them to light they are only
> assumptions on your part.

Similarly, articulating your own intentions and expectations may
help to crystallize or even define them.

Take time at the beginning of your venture to understand your
colleagues' goals, objectives, intentions, expectations, hopes,
dreams and desires for it. In addition, take the time to understand
the specific meanings of the words they use at this time, in this
context. And ensure that they understand yours as well. If you
don't, you may very well end up disappointed when your own
expectations are not met, or when you are criticized for not
satisfying someone else's.

♦ If you want to ensure alignment of purpose, dialogue – and
  use lots of it.

♦ Plus generate a documented record of agreements.

By spending time and energy to ensure that all are 'on the same
page', you and your colleagues as diverse individuals and groups
have a better chance of pulling together to create what you want.

## Neutralizing Inherent Individual and Organizational Difficulties

### Personal frame of reference

Consider what you are up against when you set out to collaborate
across organizational boundaries. First, individuality. This
represents both a potential benefit and detriment for all
collaborative efforts. Almost like luggage, you and your colleagues
all carry with you into a collaborative effort your own 'personal
truths' – your ambitions, life experiences, biases, education and
training, work experiences, cultural and ethnic backgrounds,
successes, failures, perspectives, values, beliefs, behaviors,
personalities. You bring to your work all your family joys and
sorrows, your hobbies, your relationships with friends and
colleagues. You all carry some of your personal truths consciously
and some unconsciously; some publicly and some privately.

These personal truths combine to form a unique personal

frame of reference for each person involved in the collaboration through which they view and experience the world, relationships, work and this specific venture (see Figure 2).

These personal frames of reference are important in a cross-organizational collaboration. They determine whether and how each individual judges what can or cannot be done, what is good or bad, what is easy or difficult, what works or what doesn't.

To make matters even more complicated, each participant in a collaborative venture views everyone else's frame of reference through his or her own.

> Just as sunscreen filters out ultraviolet rays from reaching your skin, personal frames of reference serve as filters on your connections with others.

Some find common ground in their frames of reference, an opening through which they can connect, while others seem to have their connections blocked. As a result, some participants seem to get along well, while others struggle to communicate, relate or get anything accomplished together.

These personal frames of reference can impact your collaborative venture both positively and negatively. To have

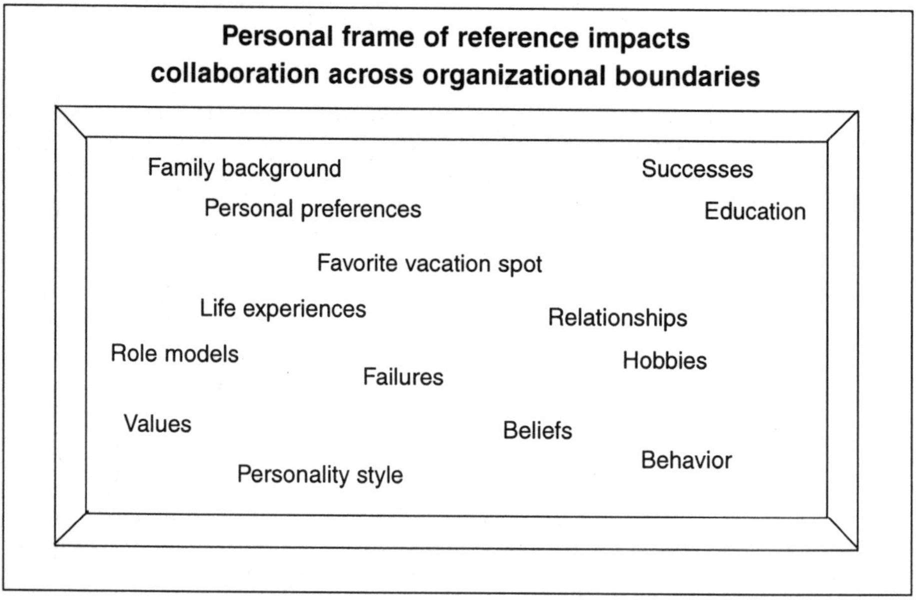

**Personal frame of reference impacts collaboration across organizational boundaries**

Family background                    Successes
Personal preferences                        Education
Favorite vacation spot
Life experiences                Relationships
Role models                                    Hobbies
Failures
Values                              Beliefs
Behavior
Personality style

Fig. 2.   Personal frame of reference.

positive impact all the personal frames of reference must fit together. Otherwise, even the good qualities of one individual can compete or conflict with the good qualities of another. And these potential difficulties may not be evident until a problem situation arises. They surface under stress and add to the difficulty.

In order to secure a common purpose in the minds and hearts of participants, you must guide the process by which participants in the collaboration 'know and become known'. By doing so you create what some call a 'background of relatedness'. You create openings in the personal frames of reference through which you and your colleagues can relate.

A useful technique is to have participants discuss those special things that make up each person's personal frame of reference. If done early in the life of the venture, participants have the opportunity to shape the collaboration in ways that make it beneficial for all. It is wise to review and set contexts for each venture even when participants have worked together before. Doing so highlights individuals' growth and change and their readiness for this venture, rather than leaving participants to rely only on old experiences and perceptions of each other.

So to make the most out of your collaborative venture, you must know the people you're dealing with:

- ◆ Who your colleagues are as people.
- ◆ What your colleagues want out of this venture.
- ◆ What your colleagues can and will do to help the venture succeed.

And your colleagues must know you.

To gain the most benefit from unique personal frames of reference, you must ensure that the venture can take advantage of the strengths and interests of each individual in a way that each can work comfortably and compatibly in relation to others involved.

### Case Study: A consulting alliance is established

Tom and Susan, two independent consultants, thought it would be useful to 'partner' to create more of a presence in the marketplace. They had a little experience working together, respected each other as colleagues, and thought they would get along fine. As part of formalizing their agreement to move forward they found it helpful to take time to get better acquainted, and to understand their personal frames of reference as highlighted in Figure 3 (below).

By going through this exercise in reasonable detail at the beginning of their venture, Tom and Susan found that while they had many things in common, they also had many important differences, which could work for or against their collaboration. By examining these they were able to form their collaboration in a way that capitalized on each person's strengths and interests, and minimized difficulties resulting from distinct preferences. Susan assumed primary responsibility for public interface while Tom took on most of the internal, behind the scenes activities. Determining an appropriate blend of private time and collaborative meeting time helped too. _____

| Personal frames of reference summary | | |
|---|---|---|
| | **Tom** | **Susan** |
| *Family influences* | ◆ Widowed mother, sister, grandmother, grandfather | ◆ Mother, father, brother, sister, grandmother |
| *Education* | ◆ Advanced degrees in engineering | ◆ Advanced degrees in science and management |
| *Hobbies and interests* | ◆ Sports and travel | ◆ Music, art, travel |
| *Preferred communication style* | ◆ Written | ◆ Verbal |
| *Favorite holiday/vacation spot* | ◆ Ocean | ◆ Mountains |
| *Preferred work environment* | ◆ Quiet, private | ◆ Meetings with people |
| *Key personal values at work* | ◆ Integrity, quality | ◆ Integrity, making a difference |
| *Scope of market interest* | ◆ United States | ◆ International |

Fig. 3.   Personal frames of reference exercise summary.

## *Organizational frame of reference*

Beyond the idiosyncrasies of individuals, special challenges become apparent when multiple organizations are involved in a collaborative effort. Add to the individuals the specifics of the organizations they are representing – their organizational frames of reference:

- ◆ Stated and unstated policies, procedures, practices and politics of the organizations involved.
- ◆ Explicit and implicit expectations of their colleagues.

These include:
- values, beliefs and guiding principles
- customs
- policies
- strategies
- organizational structure
- business practices
- procedures
- support systems and processes
- success measures.

Think about where similarities or differences may lie across organizational boundaries:

### Business strategy

Some organizations may be interested in profit while others are more interested in gaining revenue or market share. Some may be focused on growth of their own enterprise while others are looking to preserve the current base. Some may be focused on functional or technical quality of product or service at the expense of schedule or cost while others want just the opposite. Some may value long-term relationships with customers or suppliers while others are inclined to focus on short-term gains. And it is not uncommon to see different motivations even when the organizations in question are parts of the same company.

Like relatives of a bride and groom at a wedding, these differences are all present in a cross-organizational collaboration. If you don't articulate a strategy for your venture, participants will be influenced by the strategies of their individual organizations.

### People and organization structure

Some organizations have well defined policies, procedures, and practices while others have flexible or non-existent policies, procedures and practices. Some organizations grow people from within while others hire expertise and experience from the outside. In some organizations people are valued for their competence, expertise or creativity while in others people are valued for their seniority. Some organizations behave in a hierarchical way, with clear regard for title, seniority and/or authority, while others prefer democracy or anarchy as the primary form of governance.

Individuals carry to your collaborative venture these constructs of the organizations they represent. If you don't deal explicitly with the issues and reconcile the differences, individuals and organizations will rely on their own experiences to determine for themselves how this venture should operate.

### Key business processes and systems
Some organizations are fond of using voice mail to facilitate communication while others prefer email or face-to-face meetings. Some have developed their own customized computer software systems to monitor and manage their daily operations while others employ off-the-shelf software packages. Some individuals enjoy having decisions made for them while others enjoy participating in the decision-making process in their organizations on the basis of 'one vote per person'. In some organizations conflicts are dealt with head on, directly and quickly, while in others conflicts are avoided at all costs.

If you aren't explicit about the processes and systems to be used in your venture, you can bet that you will end up with some of each – potentially redundant, inefficient and costly.

### Measures of success
As stated above, some organizations focus on growth in revenue or market share as the primary measure of success, while others are more interested in maximizing short-term profitability. Some want to change the world, while others view success as offering an existing product or service better, faster, or cheaper. Even how individuals and groups are recognized and rewarded can vary dramatically across organizational boundaries.

Unless you identify specific measures of success for your collaborative venture, participants will probably assume that the ones they are committed to already apply here.

All of these areas represent sources for possible differences in values, beliefs, preferences and operational approach to collaboration.

To create a synergy and ensure a common purpose for collaboration across organizational boundaries, you have to:

- Develop a common vision regarding the desired outcome.
- Establish clear, measurable objectives and priorities.
- Manage the expectations of those involved.

**Case Study:  Two companies develop common ground** _____

In determining whether and how to collaborate, executives from two companies had to look long and hard to find how to connect. Their organizational frames of reference were quite different, as shown by examples in the table below.

| | Company A | Company B |
|---|---|---|
| *Business strategy– products and services provided in the marketplace* | ◆ Industry-focused, business-to-business direct sales | ◆ Consumer-oriented, retail |
| *Measure of profitability and success* | ◆ Long-term growth in market share | ◆ Short-term revenue and profit |
| *Operational processes and systems* | ◆ Distributed decision-making process<br>◆ Reliance on email as primary means of communication<br>◆ Home-grown computer systems for management information<br>◆ Open facilities, with many site amenities | ◆ Centralized decision-making process<br>◆ Preference for meetings and phone conversations; heavy voice mail traffic<br>◆ Industry standard, off-the-shelf computer software for management information<br>◆ Hard-wall offices, with few amenities |
| *People and organization structure* | ◆ Egalitarian mindset, with relatively flat organization model<br>◆ Stock options for all employees | Hierarchical organizational model<br>◆ Stock options only for executives |
| *Key partners and suppliers* | ◆ Many contractors, consultants and temporary employees<br>◆ Many suppliers | ◆ Few outside contractors, consultants and temporary employees<br>◆ Few suppliers |

To work together, representatives from the two companies had to develop
a common vision for the future to supersede their existing ways of
life.

Even with marked differences at the onset, collaboration can be successful
across organizational boundaries if the parties can find common ground. _____

## Understanding Context

Every collaboration across organizational boundaries exists in the
context of a bigger picture. In some cases you can control your
destiny; in others you cannot. Where circumstances are fixed, like
'stakes in the ground', articulate them. Doing so helps to clarify
definitions, assumptions and boundaries for the collaboration.
Potential 'stakes in the ground' include:

- External forces – for example government regulations, market
  conditions, competition, technological innovations, availability
  of resources in the marketplace.
- Internal constraints – for example scope, schedule, budget,
  allocation of resources.

The earlier you identify and deal with these realities the better
your chance of success. You and your colleagues will waste less
time bumping into obstacles and having to backtrack and rework.
Also, by understanding context early you can ensure that the
vision for the venture makes more sense.

**Case Study:   Timing is important** _____

In one collaborative venture the market window was only 18 months, so
schedule was critical. If those involved could not deliver within the time
constraint there was no point in proceeding.

This business context was very important for all to understand and appreciate.
Those involved in the venture crafted their common purpose to meet the
schedule requirement. _____

## Creating a Vision for Success

If you ask those who have done it what it takes for collaboration
across organizational boundaries to be successful, you find that a
clear vision regarding the desired outcome is critical. Such vision
must be either large enough to include the 'success requirements'
of all involved, or small enough to establish one common agenda,

exclusive of all other special interests. Vision regarding the desired outcome:

- Defines the playing field and the rules of the game at a high level.
- Enables all participants to align their own activities and behaviors to both preserve core beliefs and values and make progress toward the overall goal.

If you ask more detailed questions, you learn that this vision is comprised of two parts: philosophy and picture. Both are necessary; neither is sufficient on its own.

---

Vision = Philosophy + Picture

---

Philosophy includes guiding principles, values and beliefs that are held dear by the group, along with an expression of the group's fundamental motivation or primary reason for being. These capture participants' hearts and provide a level of moral guidance for participants' plans, activities and behaviors.

Picture includes a clear and compelling overall goal along with a vibrant, tangible measure of success. When it is cogent, concise and compelling, this picture serves as a unifying focal point for the effort.

Some describe their mission. Some talk about having a bold goal. Some would say that this vision for success needs to fit on a t-shirt in the form of a slogan.

---

However you label it, your vision for success must encapsulate: fundamental reason for being; guiding principles, values and beliefs; the overall goal for the venture; and a high-level measure of success.

---

As depicted in Figure 4, vision provides a high-level target for your venture. To unify and mobilize participants, combine the philosophy and picture for your venture into one short statement that expresses your principles, values and beliefs, and the overall measurable goal. Make sure it is easily understood by all involved.

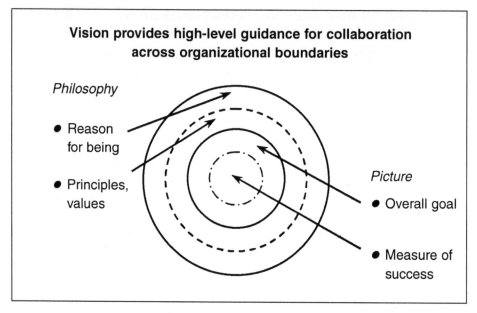

Fig. 4.    Vision.

**Case study:    Vision for a community consortium is solidified** _____

Following a series of devastating circumstances involving drugs, violence and the death of some teenagers, one community decided to take action. Elected officials from the school board, city council and hospital board wanted to consolidate their efforts to improve the situation. But how? To date, all of their individual and organizational success had been based on individual election platforms, partisan agendas and history of separate priorities and interests. Even so, the motivation for change was strong. These elected officials agreed to meet together with members of the community to create a new kind of collaboration.

Under the watchful eyes of the press, and with the help of a skilled outside facilitator, they created their vision for the future. Cross-functional discussion groups comprised of community members and elected officials from each of the three bodies developed word pictures of what success would look like if their desired change were to be realized. They presented their ideas to each other, and together created a consolidated vision – one clear, concise, compelling vision of the future that they all would commit to create. As stated in minutes from their meeting, they created:

. . . *a forum whereby the community at large will work collaboratively to promote an environment that fosters:*
*Optimal health, housing, human services*

*Total community involvement*
*Healthy leisure/recreational/cultural activities*
*Healthy economy*
*Safety*
*Sustainable physical environment.*
*'It takes a village to raise a child'.* _____

## Establishing Objectives and Priorities

Once the vision is clear, establish specific objectives and priorities for the collaboration. As one executive says, 'Here's where we nail down anything that could move.'

Some people can understand a vision and intuitively do the right thing; the challenge is how to keep them on course with others. At the same time, many people need more detail in order to move forward. They need specific marching orders.

> For collaboration to succeed, you must offer enough detailed guidance so that all involved can stay focused, productive and on course.

This is also where constraints take hold. Based on the availability of real resources you must make choices regarding scope, schedule and allocation of resources for the venture. For example, questions you should consider include:

- Of all the possibilities, how do we interpret this vision in order to develop objectives that our group can achieve?
- What are our specific deliverables?
- What interdependencies exist?
- What will we do first, second, third, etc to make our vision a reality?
- Who is accountable for what deliverables?
- What is the schedule and budget for work to be done?

Setting objectives and establishing clear priorities helps to solidify purpose and manage everyone's expectations – What will be accomplished? By whom? By when?

Take the time to clarify understanding, develop commitment and document these objectives and priorities. The consolidated list of objectives and priorities represents an important agreement for the collaboration.

In many dynamic, complex ventures it is almost impossible to cast in concrete every detail that is necessary for individuals to behave autonomously over the duration of the venture. As a result, you must:

- Ensure that efforts can be coordinated.
- Create a forum for dialogue to check for alignment among participants on an ongoing basis.

That way objectives and priorities can be reviewed and realigned as needed over the life of the collaboration. To coordinate efforts and check for alignment you can use regular meetings with clear agenda, one-to-one conversations, and/or the familiar 'management by walking around'.

### Case study:   A $250 million business is launched

By pulling together key representatives from sales, service and engineering, and aligning their objectives and priorities, one high tech company improved collaboration across organizational boundaries and paved the way for a successful new business.

Board members and senior management were focused on the need for increased profitability and enhanced reputation for the company as they agreed to launch a new line of business. The vision was to be 'better, faster, cheaper' than the company's main competitor.

Separately, each of the three functional organizations had their own expectations for what 'success' would look like:

| Sales | Service | Engineering |
|---|---|---|
| ◆ Low product price | ◆ Product reliability | ◆ Product introduction in one year |
| ◆ Product introduction within six months | ◆ Maintainability | ◆ Freedom of product design |
| ◆ Competitive features | ◆ Low cost of product maintenance | ◆ Technological innovation |
| ◆ Special packaging and aesthetics | ◆ Distinct support and auxiliary services | ◆ Peer recognition |

Objectives and priorities had to be set to motivate all involved, while reconciling differences and clarifying aspects so that all participants could understand and commit to achieving what was expected of them – for example:

- Specifically what product features are needed and why?

- What do we mean by 'low price' and 'low cost'?
- How much and what kind of technological innovation is appropriate?
- What date will this group commit for product introduction?
- How do we reconcile the opposing expected benefit from a particular feature with the forecasted increased cost of maintenance?

Working together across organizational boundaries this team clarified specific objectives and priorities. Key to their discussion and decision-making regarding objectives and priorities were:

- High-level functional specification document – describing the features and functions to be provided.
- Technical specification document – defining how product features and functions would be implemented, and itemizing costs.
- Integrated product plan, schedule, and budget – showing milestones, interdependencies and critical path; and eliminating redundancies while ensuring holistic picture of all that would be important for this venture to succeed.
- Market analysis summary and business justification – positioning this venture with respect to potential customers, competitors and other market forces.
- Regular core team meetings – enabling communication and developing both individual and functional commitment to the venture. _____

## Key Tools and Techniques

Alignment of purpose is critical for successful collaboration across organizational boundaries. A common purpose serves as a fundamental unifying force for those involved in the collaboration by providing:

- Overall direction and focus.
- Defined freedoms and boundaries.
- High-level moral guidance and ideals.

To ensure alignment of purpose:

- ✔ Engage in dialogue with participants early and often to ensure common meanings and expectations.
- ✔ Record agreements so that there is a documented reference point when memories fade or recall things differently.
- ✔ Acknowledge and build on the personal and organizational frames of reference for all involved in the collaboration.

✔ Articulate the context in which your collaborative venture exists.

✔ Establish and document guiding principles by which those involved will live.

✔ Ensure that there is a clear, concise and compelling vision of the desired outcome.

✔ Document specific objectives and priorities as a form of agreement.

✔ Create a forum to coordinate efforts and check for alignment on a regular basis.

CHAPTER 3

# Ability to Perform

Nothing squashes collaboration across organizational boundaries quite like poor performance. Poor performance by individuals or organizations in a collaborative venture:

◆ Delays results.
◆ Undermines trust and respect of others involved in the collaboration.
◆ Distracts participants while they wonder and worry about what is (not) going on.

To build successful collaboration across organizational boundaries you must ensure that every person and organization performs – in their respective roles, in your venture. A tall order.

In order to guarantee performance you need to consider:

◆ The people and organizations involved – their skills, talents, interests and whether/how they fit in this venture.
◆ The jobs to be done – accountabilities, boundaries, interdependencies, etc.
◆ The construct of the collaboration itself – issues of governance, inherent pressures, constraints.

All of these play a role in whether and how individuals and organizations can and will perform.

## Engaging the Right People – Function/Form/Fit

Regardless of the type of collaborative venture you are a part of, you must concern yourself with having the right people involved. 'Right' in terms of:

◆ The abilities of the individuals to perform the required **functions**.
◆ The way (**form**) in which the individuals do their work.
◆ Whether and how each individual **fits** as part of your venture.

## Function

Think about how you select participants for a collaborative venture. What do you look for? What criteria do you use to decide that 'this organization is perfect' or 'that individual is not appropriate for this venture'? Many look for technical or functional expertise first and foremost when embarking on a collaborative venture. They look for the 'best' to be part of their team – the world-renowned heart surgeon, the most sought after software graphical user interface designer, the most publicized contemporary architectural firm, the most published professor, the most profitable global manufacturing company, etc. They look for knowledge, skills, reputation, accomplishments, interest and passion all around particular content.

Yet those experienced in successful business partnering relationships across organizational boundaries know that content expertise alone is not enough. Content expertise does not ensure that an individual or organization will be effective in a collaborative venture or that the venture will be successful because of the content expert's participation. After all, by its very nature collaboration implies that individuals and organizations work together. That means that process expertise – how individuals and organizations go about their work with others – is needed too. What make the difference in successful cross-organizational collaborations are participants' abilities to both accomplish tasks and manage relationships with others.

As shown in Figure 5, you need a wide spectrum of skills and behaviors to accomplish tasks and manage relationships effectively. If you and your colleagues err on the side of only accomplishing the tasks, you may as well work alone. Likewise, if you or they err on the side of only engaging in relationship with each other, you are not likely to add any unique value to the venture.

So you must consider the *nature* of your venture. When tasks are simple and handoffs between individuals and organizations are clean and straightforward, collaboration among those who only accomplish tasks may work. Most often, however, things are not that easy. Tasks are complex and require work from more than one individual or organization, and handoffs between individuals and organizations require coordination and communication.

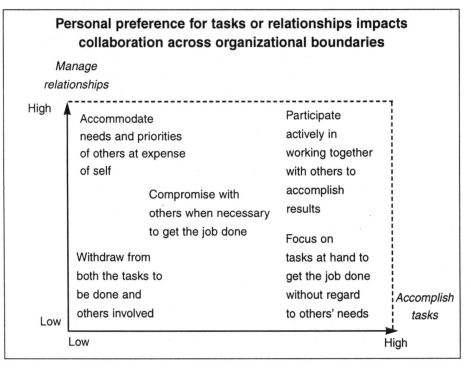

**Personal preference for tasks or relationships impacts collaboration across organizational boundaries**

*Manage relationships*

High — Accommodate needs and priorities of others at expense of self

Participate actively in working together with others to accomplish results

Compromise with others when necessary to get the job done

Focus on tasks at hand to get the job done without regard to others' needs — *Accomplish tasks*

Withdraw from both the tasks to be done and others involved

Low

Low — High

Fig. 5.   Balancing tasks and relationships.

Hence a balance of content and process is required for collaboration to be successful.

We all have a predisposition regarding whether we spend our time accomplishing tasks or managing relationships. You must find the right mix of participants for your venture. Consider your own usual behavior and that of your colleagues. There is not just one magic formula. If you are now selecting participants for a new collaborative venture or trying to energize an existing venture, consider the appropriate balance of task and relationship for your specific venture.

Checklist

To help you examine your own skills and behaviors and those of your colleagues, here is a checklist that some have found helpful in searching for those individuals and organizations that are effective in business partnering relationships:

◆ Functional competence – appropriate level for the work to be done.

◆ Fluency in the 'language' of the venture – proficiency with jargon, acronyms, colloquialisms unique to the venture.

- Clear role to play on the team – specific accountabilities and deliverables.
- Personal passion for the work – how much a person likes their work and its impact on others.
- Service mentality – the level to which a person wants to support and collaborate with others.
- Cultural fit.
- Wise use of power – how well a person uses their professional expertise, positional authority and personal character for the good of the venture.
- 'Welcome' factor – how well a person is accepted by others in a group as a leader or a group member.

**Case study:   'I'll take teamwork first'** _____

John is an executive with more than 20 years' experience in initiating and guiding business partnering relationships across organizational boundaries. He has led both large and small projects with cross-organizational teams comprised of participants from different departments within his company as well as from outside the company. In addition, he has crafted ongoing business partnering relationships involving multiple companies.

In his words: 'What I found out through our experiences with partnering is that content knowledge is not the only factor for success. In fact, sometimes having a team member that is content rich without having the understanding and characteristics of teamwork and good partnering behavior can actually achieve less than the ideal outcome. It is actually better to optimize the team. Rather than having a team member who is an 'A' player in content and a 'C' or 'D' player in teamwork, I would select a 'B' player in content who is an 'A' or 'B' player in teamwork. A team member who is 'B' and 'B' will be more effective than one who is 'A' and 'C'. Even though you might think it would average out, it doesn't. The ability of the team to work together is critical. Even if a person has excellent content knowledge, if he or she cannot transmit the knowledge or influence others, that knowledge is not excellent for us. All the ingredients of partnering have to be there for success. If we need additional technical expertise we can contract for it as needed for a particular task, not as an ongoing part of the partnering relationship.

What I really look for is 'A' content knowledge and 'A' partnering skills. Through interview and reference checking I look for team members who are collaborative, have demonstrated ability to influence others, present holistic analysis, and come to the venture with open minds.' _____

## *Form*

As you are selecting participants for a cross-organizational collaboration, or as you are trying to understand why such a business venture is or is not working, you must examine form – that is, how you and your colleagues go about doing your work. Day to day behavior is a good indicator of how well or poorly cross-organizational collaborations perform. Your interpersonal behavior, moment by moment, is impacted by how much each of you wants to be in charge and how much you want to be accepted and included by others. These personal needs for control and belonging impact your collaboration with others.

Consider your own tendencies. In general, do you prefer to take the lead in a business situation or to submit to the guidance of your boss or colleagues? Whichever you choose, do you do so cheerfully, with a personal desire to cooperate with others, or somewhat grudgingly, hoping to make others wrong in the end?

Now consider the usual behaviors of your colleagues:

♦ Do they typically take the lead or fall in line with the group?
♦ Do they do so cooperatively or reluctantly?

Your answers to these questions can offer a lot of insight about the nature of your collaboration. For example, the more you and your colleagues want to cooperate with each other, the more natural and comfortable the partnering relationship is likely to feel. Similarly, the more alone participants prefer to be, the more difficult the partnering is likely to be.

At the same time, the more would-be leaders there are in your venture, the more attention needs to be paid to gaining agreement on the rules of engagement for the venture – that is, specific roles, responsibilities, policies and procedures. Otherwise, all the leaders are likely to take charge in their own unique ways.

Your answers to the questions above may be 'Well, it depends . . .'. So the form your collaborative venture takes *does* depend on lots of factors, including:

- Innate personal behaviors of each participant, and individual perspectives of each about the others.
- Importance of the venture to all concerned, and the abilities of all participants to be on their 'good' behavior.
- Expectations of each participant with respect to how things should operate.
- Explicit agreements among participants as to protocol for this venture.
- Consequences to each participant resulting from inappropriate behavior.

As a result, for your collaboration to be successful you need to understand something about how individuals in the venture behave. Doing so offers guidance about your own behavior and points you in a direction to use behavior that will be received well by your colleagues.

**Case study:   Paul learns the meaning of collaboration** _____

Paul is a very bright engineer. He is known for doing good work. He is creative, dependable, results-oriented. He can be counted on to meet his commitments. He is self-sufficient, and does not require a lot of support or help from his colleagues. He is skilled at understanding customers' needs and his boss's requirements, and is able to satisfy both on a regular basis. As an individual contributor Paul is held in high regard by all who work with him.

It was when Paul was assigned a leadership role managing a team as part of a worldwide cross-functional effort that he had to learn to really collaborate. He found that his technical expertise and his ability to deliver results to his boss were required, but not sufficient to be successful in this venture.

In his words, 'Things seem to be swirling more. They are not nice and neat. I have to keep other people informed about what I'm doing. It's not enough to complete my tasks. It definitely impacts my way of working. Others want more information from me on an ongoing basis.'

At first Paul was uncomfortable with, and even a little resentful of these new demands. He looked at the need for more communication and coordination with others as both distrust by others of his abilities and a waste of his time. However, as he adapted his own work habits to include more communication and coordination with others, remaining 'in relationship with' his colleagues, Paul became even more successful. _____

## *Fit*

To ensure that the 'right' people are involved in the venture you must consider also whether or not what they offer is what the venture really needs. Just like in cooking, the ingredients have to work together. You must look at each participant in relation to the others. If they don't mesh well together, neither will your venture.

### Case study:   Extra costs for software development

In one fast-track computer software development venture involving three companies, the leaders had to look twice at assignments of people.

At the beginning of the venture, leaders from all three companies assigned the necessary number of software engineers who were 'bright and experienced'. Without careful scrutiny of the skills and interests of assigned personnel or thorough discussion of roles and responsibilities of participants from the three companies:

- scope of the effort was defined
- schedule and budget were set
- tasks were assigned
- software development began.

It was only when key deadlines became jeopardized, and costs for the venture began to escalate beyond the plan, that the leaders from the three companies worked together to look more carefully at personnel. They found:

### Function

- All of the software engineers were in fact 'experienced', with mixed reputations based on their prior assignments.
- All of the software engineers were 'familiar' with the computer software languages and protocols to be used, but not all had sufficient background and experience with the advanced features that were important to this effort.
- The combined team was lacking in sufficient technical problem-solving skills, necessary for trouble-shooting and in software engineering know-how necessary for creating innovative software solutions.

### Form

- Most of the software engineers were 'nice guys' who complied with the leaders' requests.

♦ One of the more senior engineers persisted in disrupting meetings and in frustrating others by his lack of accountability for deliverables of any kind.

♦ One of the more junior engineers continually told leaders that 'things were fine', instead of asking for assistance when he needed it.

**Fit**

♦ The combined team had more senior software engineers and senior staff than needed, and not enough talented doers. This contributed to higher costs and more management time to reconcile different points of view regarding how to proceed.

The desired short development schedule was compromised by the lack of functional capability. In addition, extra management time was required to manage disruptive behavior, deal with unnecessary conflicts, and constantly monitor and track progress at the detail level.

Senior management decided to reassign three of the software engineers and bring in others who were better suited for the job. This cost the venture both in terms of lost productivity and the need to retrain new engineers. The good news is that senior management caught these problems in time, and even with the extra costs involved, the venture proved successful.   _____

## Clarifying Roles, Responsibilities and Accountabilities

The guidance here is to 'nail down anything that can move'. Consistent with good business practice, you will find that people perform better when they know what is expected of them. In addition, in a collaborative venture it is important for all to know what they can and should expect from each other.

> That's the key – expectations in relationship to each other.

Also, successful collaboration across organizational boundaries means crossing 'white space', that space between boxes on organizational charts. This white space is an important place, because it represents the space where things can get lost, where familiar rules may not apply, and where there exists a wealth of opportunity for individuals and organizations to be creative.

If roles, responsibilities and accountabilities are not well defined, participants in your venture will make assumptions. Some of those will be right and others will be wrong. This can impact performance unfavorably as participants become disappointed in their colleagues.

Many techniques are effective in clarifying roles, responsibilities and accountabilities for participants in a business partnering relationship. These include:

♦ Abbreviated forms of a standard job description for each participant.
♦ Ongoing dialogue among participants.
♦ Documented minutes from working meetings articulating who is doing what to whom.
♦ Roles and responsibilities matrix, indicating for key deliverables and activities who:
  – is accountable for the outcome/drives the process
  – contributes to the work/supports the effort
  – must be kept informed along the way
  – has decision-making authority/approval authority.

**Case study:  Clear ownership makes collaborative strategic planning easier** _____

In one worldwide organization, strategic planning was defined as a collaborative activity involving all the independent business units and functional departments. To make this work roles, responsibilities and authority levels had to be clear for all involved. Some activities needed to be owned by the independent business units; others by the corporate functions. Similarly, some things required approval from the CEO or board of directors (BOD); others could be authorized by business unit general managers (GM) or functional vice presidents (VP).

After representatives from all organizations developed and applied the matrix shown in Figure 6 (page 42) the global process worked smoothly.

Key to this successful collaborative strategic planning process were:

♦ Clear ownership/accountability for outcomes.
♦ One final authority/decision maker.
♦ Knowing who needed to be involved to contribute along the way versus who needed to be kept informed. _____

| Strategic planning process collaboration matrix | | | | | | | | | |
|---|---|---|---|---|---|---|---|---|---|
| Key task/ deliverable | Strat. planning VP | Finance VP | Bus. unit Ops A GM | Bus. unit Ops B GM | Bus. unit Ops C GM | Corp. function 1 VP | Corp. function 2 VP | COO | CEO/ BOD |
| *Annual worldwide corporate strategic business plan* | O | C | C | C | C | C | C | C | A |
| *Business unit plans and performance* | I | I | O | O | O | C | C | A | I |
| *Business justification* | C | C | O | O | O | C | C | C | A |
| *Financial analysis and modelling* | I | O/A | C | C | C | I | I | I | – |
| *Long-term scenario planning* | O | C | C | C | C | C | C | C | A |
| *Functional support plans and performance* | I | I | C | C | C | O | O | A | – |
| *Short-term tactical plans* | I | C | O | O | O | O | O | I | – |
| **Legend:**<br>O: Is accountable for **outcome**<br>C: **Contributes** to the work<br>I: Must be kept **informed**<br>A: Has decision-making **authority** | | | | | | | | | |

Fig. 6.   Sample roles and responsibilities matrix.

## Managing Fuzzy Boundaries

Not everything in the workplace is nice and neat. As a result, special attention must be paid to managing 'fuzzy boundaries' – fuzzy boundaries with respect to roles, responsibilities, authorities and ultimate individual and organizational performance in your collaborative venture. These include:

- ◆ Overlapping roles and responsibilities.
- ◆ New ways of doing things for new situations.
- ◆ Opportunities for innovation.
- ◆ Getting the job done on a daily basis.

Any of these conditions may exist by design or by accident. For example, there will be times when, regardless of good intentions to minimize redundancy and clarify assignments, more than one person will think he or she is responsible for the same thing. Likewise, circumstances will dictate that you try a new or different approach. Breakthroughs in technology or methodology will offer opportunities for innovation. And, sometimes, a third hand will be required just to get the job done.

> Because they call on individuals to make choices about how they behave, these fuzzy boundaries test the very essence of partnering. Whether and how you and your colleagues manage these fuzzy boundaries is an indicator of how well your team is able to perform.

**Case study:   Serving customers is everyone's responsibility**_____

In a global company with organizational boundaries formed both geographically by country and functionally by business units, telephone calls from customers can come to many people in the company – a local sales or customer service representative, an engineer in a business unit, the manufacturing manager who gave a presentation during a customer briefing, a financial analyst responsible for billing or accounts receivable, a receptionist, an executive at the company's headquarters location, etc. As a result, the boundary regarding who deals with customers is fuzzy.

Rather than put too many unnecessary restrictions on the company's customers, the company has focused its effort on making sure that calls from customers are handled well. The company's guiding principle of 'Put customers first' serves the cross-organizational collaboration. _____

# Developing a Core Team

In most business partnering relationships you will not be able to have every participant involved directly in every decision. Size and complexity of the venture dictate that you must create some form of government. Most find a **core team** to be effective in this role.

A core team comprises a manageable number of key representatives of the principal organizations involved in the venture, ensuring some organizational or contractual relationship with every participant in the venture.

Key responsibilities for the core team include:

- direction setting
- operational coordination
- problem escalation.

In short, the core team provides leadership for the venture.

**Case study:   A $60 million venture gets off to a good start**_____

As part of the planning for one collaborative venture involving three companies for a period of 18 months, a core team was formed with two executives from each of the companies. Initially this core team convened to determine how they would measure success for the venture. Their dialogue to establish success criteria took place during three meetings, allowing time for these core team members to digest each conversation and understand the implications of their agreements. Through this explicit process, these executives:

- Became better acquainted and comfortable with each other by sharing their philosophies, experiences, plans and concerns.
- Created a common language for this venture, by clarifying meanings and choosing words that made sense to all involved.
- Developed a definition for success which all could support.

This core team decided on the following success criteria for their collaborative venture:

- 'Business objectives, schedule and budget are met.
- The team establishes and maintains an effective communication process throughout the life of the venture.
- The venture is a financial success for all parties.
- This venture creates a model for future success in terms of learnings, reference and pride.

◆ Every team member involved in the venture has a sense of personal satisfaction.
◆ This venture is fun.'

In addition, this core team agreed to convene on a monthly basis to ensure that they would stay on course to achieve their desired success. _____

## Managing Performance

Once you have established criteria for success you need some way to monitor and influence performance on an ongoing basis. How you monitor and manage performance says a lot about the nature of your collaboration. For example:

◆ Who judges performance? Is performance management the duty of one or more leaders or does the whole team have a role in evaluating and guiding performance? In true partnering relationships, all participants have a vested interest in the success of the whole. Hence it is incumbent upon everyone to be able to give and receive performance feedback within appropriate contexts and spheres of influence, and it is important to have a collaborative approach to performance management – something that all support.

◆ What do you focus on to monitor performance? Do you focus on accomplishments or problems? Performance is linked positively to praise. Good performance builds on itself when recognized and rewarded. Therefore your ability to focus on achievement is key. You must provide positive feedback in addition to criticism. For collaboration to grow, you must recognize and reward the behavior that you want.

◆ When do you monitor and manage performance? Are you proactive, monitoring performance on an ongoing basis or do you wait until 'stuff' happens? Waiting until problems escalate in order to take action destroys collaboration. As stated earlier, this undermines trust and respect among participants, and distracts participants from getting real work accomplished. Your willingness to be proactive contributes to building successful collaboration.

◆ Where do you monitor performance? Do you have a formal, automated system that supplies the group with reports, charts and graphs, or do you conduct informal conversations with those involved? Whatever you choose, gain agreement among those involved as to which approach is best for your venture.

There are lots of acceptable ways to monitor and manage performance. Selected means and mechanisms are described in more detail in Chapter 4. The trick is to gain agreement among those involved as to which approach is right for your venture, and then to apply your chosen approach faithfully.

**Case study:   Progress reporting helps to manage performance** _____

Participants in one collaborative venture chose to convene monthly for formal progress reviews. 'Stand and Deliver' they called their meetings. Two hours in length, these meetings helped to formalize communication among eight organizations, celebrate accomplishments and focus attention on next steps. Their meeting notice read as follows:

*Stand and Deliver Meeting Notice*

| | |
|---|---|
| Date: | Monday, February 14 |
| Time: | 7:30 am – 11:30 am PST |
| Location: | Building A, Conference Room 1 |
| Participants: | 10 Core Team members plus list |
| Agenda: | |
| 80 min. | – 10-minute presentations from eight organizations |

- Highlights – top two key accomplishments since last meeting
- Lowlights – greatest difficulty since last meeting
- Learnings – most important thing learned since last meeting
- Radar – top two things to count on from this group by next meeting
- Heads up – any issues/concerns that the group should be aware of

| | |
|---|---|
| 20 min. | – Break |
| 40 min. | – Confirm priorities/check for alignment |
| 60 min. | – Brainstorm – mitigation of issues/concerns by priority |
| 40 min. | – Action planning. _____ |

## Getting the Performance You Want

> Please remember that in context all behaviors make sense.

If individuals or organizations are not performing according to your expectations it is probably because of one or more of the following reasons:

- They do not know **what** to do.
- They do not know **how** to do it.
- There is a reason **why** they cannot do it.
- They **will** not do it because they do not want to do it.

In any case, depending on your action, you can have direct influence on performance.

### What

If participants do not know what to do, you can help clarify direction. Often misunderstanding or misinterpretation is involved when this is the case. If so, go back to the purpose of the venture, respective roles, responsibilities, priorities – even tasks if needed – to ensure that all involved know what they are being counted on to contribute.

### How

If participants do not know how to perform the tasks at hand or to accomplish the objectives, they may have inadequate knowledge or training. To improve the situation, you can help develop their skills. In some cases you must explicitly train others in how to do the job in your venture, or coach them as they grapple with things in your venture's specific context.

Many times in collaborative ventures across organizational boundaries, the situation is not that others are not doing something, or that they are doing things wrong; rather it is that they are doing things differently from how you would do them. Key examples of where others might not meet your expectations include their:

- decision-making
- documentation and reporting

- communication
- problem solving and escalation.

When this happens you must revisit process for your venture – the 'how to'. While some executives would wish this away, your willingness to spend time helping others be successful will ultimately pay dividends for your venture. The challenge is finding the appropriate balance between high-level guidance for all involved and the need for detailed policies, procedures and instructions.

## Why

Sometimes participants cannot perform because one or more obstacles are in their way. Such obstacles can be physical or conceptual. One prime example of this difficulty can be found in rewards and recognition. Often, guidance for a cross-organizational venture is promoting teamwork across organizational boundaries; at the same time, compensation for individuals or organizations is awarded based on individual achievement. This presents a real obstacle to collaboration. Because compensation is an important part of the work experience, teamwork goes out of the window in favor of individual achievement. The notion of sharing risk and reward is discussed further in Chapter 6.

While the issues regarding compensation are fairly clear, other obstacles may be subtler or not quite so visible – for example, policies, procedures, customary practice, peer pressure, etc. You must remain on the lookout for potential obstacles to collaboration and help to remove them as quickly as possible.

## Will

If personal or organizational agenda is impeding performance you have to determine whether you have the appropriate organizations and individuals involved in your collaborative venture. Of all the potential performance difficulties this is the most challenging to overcome – almost like asking a duck to become a giraffe. You may have to replace individuals or entire organizations. If that is not possible, you may have to ask your colleagues to replace you.

# Key Tools and Techniques

Performance is key to successful collaboration across organizational boundaries. To ensure that those in your venture can and will perform:

✔ Match skills and interests of both the individuals and organizations with the jobs to be done.

✔ Set clear performance expectations for each organization and each individual involved in your venture.

✔ Clarify roles, responsibilities, and accountabilities of both individuals and organizations in order to minimize both redundancies and gaps.

✔ Develop a cross-organizational core team to monitor and manage performance throughout the life of your venture.

✔ Ensure that participants balance completing their assigned tasks with staying in relationship with others so that their work makes sense in relation to the entire effort.

✔ Monitor performance regularly and make mid-course corrections as needed to ensure that participants:
  – know what to do
  – know how to do what is expected of them
  – are not impeded in any way by obstacles
  – will perform as intended.

CHAPTER 4

# Attention to Process

As the old saying goes, success is in the details. Whether you and your colleagues will create and maintain successful collaboration across organizational boundaries depends in part on how you go about your work together. It depends on how well you articulate and adhere to the key processes for your venture – the systematic series of actions you and your colleagues use to achieve some end – the 'rules' by which you work.

You and your colleagues all bring your individual experiences and personal preferences to the venture regarding how you do things. Things like how you make decisions; how you solve problems or resolve conflicts. Some of these are conscious and some you just use out of habit, almost unconsciously. Left to yourselves, you all will rely on those familiar, trusted methods to govern how you do things wherever you are.

When you introduce more than one organization to the venture, you introduce multiple organizations' ways of doing things. You will find both similarities and differences in how different organizations conduct business.

> Some will call on their policies or procedures to get things done; others will refer to their guiding principles.

However they are labeled, and whatever their significance, these 'rules' describe how people conduct business in these organizations. In addition, you will be faced with all the undocumented processes – sometimes, the real ways things work. And even when the organizations are part of the same company, subtle differences can exist in how things are done.

## Defining Process

So whose rules apply?

> To ensure successful collaboration you and your colleagues must take time to articulate how your specific collaborative relationship will operate.

Successful collaborators in many different industries and situations repeatedly point to the following as fundamental to their success:

- How to get along with each other.
- How to solve problems and resolve conflicts.
- How to stay focused on the important things.
- How to run meetings well.
- How to make and follow through on decisions.
- How to divide up the work.

For some, definition of process is the most important part of developing and maintaining successful collaboration. To them a purpose is only academic until the 'how to' is determined. Similarly, whether and how they establish trust and confidence in their colleagues is dependent on seeing and experiencing how things are going to work in the venture. Who is doing what to whom, when, and where, is critical for them to be productive, positive contributors to the collaborative venture. They want, and even need, to know the rules in order to proceed. Perhaps you are like this. If so, you know how important it is to establish governance so that all can work in harmony.

Perhaps your own priorities are different. You may be fine with a rough idea of how things should work. You may be able to move forward confidently, trusting your colleagues to do the right thing. If so, please remember that some of your colleagues require clearly defined processes in order for the collaboration to work. This means that in order to be a successful collaborator, you too need to pay attention to process.

## Making Milestones Visible

Once you have the purpose clearly defined for your venture, and that purpose has been translated into individual and group goals and objectives to which you and your colleagues have committed, you need to make those commitments public – to create and publish a documented record of your plan. Doing so serves collaboration in three ways:

♦ It keeps the group focused on what is important – what must be done by whom, when.
♦ It clarifies interdependencies among the parties – relationships between activities and milestones, and relationships between people and organizations.
♦ It manages expectations – reminding all involved what is supposed to happen when, and who is supposed to be involved.

You should update this record with actual accomplishments on an ongoing basis as you monitor your progress, shift priorities and celebrate your success.

Depending on your preference for format and ongoing administration, a number of tools and techniques exist that can help you. These include:

♦ Business planning tools and techniques such as strategic business planning, goal setting, and budgeting.
♦ Project planning tools and techniques such as Gantt charts (refer to sample in Figure 7) and PERT (Program Evaluation and Review Technique) and/or CPM (Critical Path Method)

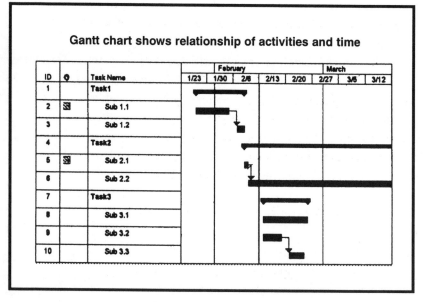

**Gantt chart shows relationship of activities and time**

| ID | ⚙ | Task Name | February | | | March | | | | |
|---|---|---|---|---|---|---|---|---|---|---|
| | | | 1/23 | 1/30 | 2/6 | 2/13 | 2/20 | 2/27 | 3/5 | 3/12 |
| 1 | | Task1 | | | | | | | | |
| 2 | ▨ | Sub 1.1 | | | | | | | | |
| 3 | | Sub 1.2 | | | | | | | | |
| 4 | | Task2 | | | | | | | | |
| 5 | ▨ | Sub 2.1 | | | | | | | | |
| 6 | | Sub 2.2 | | | | | | | | |
| 7 | | Task3 | | | | | | | | |
| 8 | | Sub 3.1 | | | | | | | | |
| 9 | | Sub 3.2 | | | | | | | | |
| 10 | | Sub 3.3 | | | | | | | | |

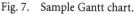

Fig. 7.   Sample Gantt chart.

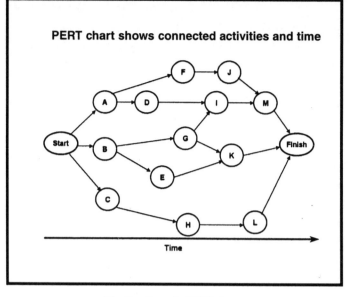

Fig. 8.   Sample PERT chart.

charts (refer to sample PERT chart in Figure 8).
- Ongoing correspondence such as meeting minutes, 'to do' lists or summary of action items highlighting who, what, by when.

Whatever you choose, select a tool or technique that makes sense to you and your colleagues, one that you will commit to use throughout the life of your venture and which you will incorporate into your daily routine to help you maintain visibility on key milestones. You want to incorporate it into your work in such a way that you can:
- Monitor progress in all key aspects of the venture.
- Foresee and avoid or minimize the impact of difficulties along the way.
- Know when and where to shift resources – up or down.
- Celebrate significant achievements.

One caution. You do not want to become a victim of your tool or technique. It should help you to maintain perspective regarding the context and big picture of your venture. Some change their plans continuously, creating new 'baselines'. After a while they find themselves way off track from the original objective, wondering how they got there. Unless you shift direction in a major way, or your plan is so messed up that no one can make sense of it, your baseline plan should be left intact throughout the life of your venture. Yes, you may fall behind your schedule, or you may take detours off the set path, but you can represent these as actual updates to the plan (plan versus actual), rather than create a new plan.

### Case study:   Movable wall panels provide visibility for successful completion

For one 18-month venture involving 25 organizations the core team identified 800 major milestones to be achieved over 18 months. These milestones were critically scrutinized, sized and shaped, and oriented in relation to each other. Members of the core team were assigned as primary owners for each of the milestones to coordinate requisite tasks and ensure on-time completion. For each milestone the following information was documented:

| Number | Milestone to be accomplished | Primary owner | Estimated resources FTE/time | Date to be completed | Must be preceded by milestone(s) # | Must precede milestone(s) # |
|---|---|---|---|---|---|---|
| | | | | | | |

Next, these milestones were placed on a calendar, to:
- Reconcile interdependencies, completion dates and resource requirements.
- Identify the 'critical path' for the venture – the sequence of connected milestones requiring the longest time.

A large PERT chart was created with the 18-month calendar running across the top, and the 25 organizations listed down the left side. Identified by their numbers, milestones owned by each of the organizations were posted according to the desired completion dates, and with connecting lines appropriately between them. Similar in form to the one shown earlier in Figure 8, this chart comprised four wall panels, each four feet wide and six feet high. The critical path for the venture was highlighted. Additionally, a movable date line was attached to quickly highlight the current date.

Preparing this chart took a lot of work, but the payoff was significant. This impressive four-panel display was used as a visual aid for meetings, and as a tangible reminder for participants regarding their respective contributions to the venture's success. As milestones were accomplished, orange dots were pasted next to the milestones on the display. At a glance all could see what was going on in the venture – what was on track, ahead or behind schedule; where the issues were; who was likely to need help; how the group was doing against the critical path. Their meetings were productive, recognizing success along the way and focusing their attention on the important issues.

Without changing the baseline plan, the group maintained complete visibility regarding what they committed to accomplish. They moved forward together. __

## Managing Relationships

At the conclusion of one collaborative venture involving several companies, the nine core team members identified the importance of managing relationships. When asked what they had learned about partnering these core team members reported:

'The partnering process itself must be managed. A core team must be established as early as possible and convene regularly to manage action items and resolve problems. Quality resources, both management and operations, from all organizations must be dedicated to support the core team. Clear lines of communication and decision making must be created and maintained.'

The same core team went on to describe the personal behavior required by all participants to ensure collaborative business relationships:

'In addition, all individuals must enhance their own personal behavior to be good partners:

- Delegate as appropriate, but take ownership and responsibility.
- Look for solutions, not excuses.
- Know your customer.
- Understand the needs, requirement and roles of other team members.
- Share knowledge among team members.
- Be proactive.
- Be open-minded.
- Have the will and commitment to 'make it happen'.
- Say what you mean, and do what you say.
- Learn to trust others even though it may be tough on you.
- Focus on the team.'

All of these qualities helped the individuals to build and maintain trust and confidence in each other, and to enjoy working together.

Also, it is important to note that some can develop effective relationships and maintain their trust and confidence in others while concentrating on the business tasks to be performed, just working alongside their colleagues over a period of time. Others need various forms of interaction to establish their personal knowledge, experience and appreciation of their colleagues' professional expertise and personal character qualities. These participants often prefer to incorporate some social time with their colleagues, creating a relaxed atmosphere where they can get to know each other better. These preferences vary according to individuals, and across organizational and cultural boundaries.

To ensure successful collaboration, you must pay attention to creating and sustaining effective relationships among people. You do not have to ensure that all are best friends; however, you do need to focus on developing a level of trust, confidence and comfort among participants so that the work can be accomplished.

### Case study:   Lack of follow through hurts business partnering relationship _____

At the beginning of one 12-month alliance, principals from the three companies involved met to:

◆ Establish common purpose, goals, objectives and priorities.

◆ Agree on the ground rules for how the venture would operate.

◆ Obtain individual and corporate commitments for moving forward.

Adequate care was taken to support this group's social needs in addition to concentrating on the work at hand. All was well. Participants from all three companies were engaged, enthusiastic and excited about working together. They spoke highly of each other. They were proud to be associated with the venture.

At the end of 12 months, the same group reported mixed results. At some levels the venture was a success. The task objectives were completed on time and within budget. Yet participants were unhappy with the experience – dissatisfied with their colleagues' adherence to the previously agreed ground rules for partnering, and disappointed in the difficulties they had experienced in working together.

When questioned, the principals admitted to not holding each other accountable for their commitments to the venture. As a group they failed to play by their own rules. What had begun as a vibrant business partnering relationship was left to flounder because of lack of follow through. _____

# Making Meetings Count

By definition, collaboration across organizational boundaries requires some number of meetings and conference calls – group interactions. Yet many complain that these meetings and conference calls are a waste of time. Complaints include:

+ too long
+ lack of preparation
+ wrong participants
+ Inadequate agenda
+ poor time management
+ discourteous behavior
+ ineffective follow-up.

You have a choice. You too can complain about ineffective and inefficient meetings, or you can create meetings that are effective and efficient. You actually can have meetings that are valuable for the venture – meetings that satisfy both individual and organizational expectations to set direction, solve problems and resolve conflicts, create innovative solutions and celebrate success.

> Make it your business to conduct and participate in valuable meetings.

Key considerations for holding valuable meetings include:

+ What is the purpose of this meeting? What would be lost if the meeting does not take place?
+ Who do you need to have in the meeting? What is each participant's role, and how do you know that they know what is expected of them?
+ What preparation is required of the participants? How much lead time do they need to prepare adequately?
+ What is the desired outcome for each agenda item?
+ Who will moderate/facilitate the meeting to ensure that it begins and ends on time, that the agenda is covered appropriately, and that the group stays focused productively?
+ Who will be responsible to take notes and ensure that a summary of agreements and action items is published following the meeting?

## *Purpose*

To encourage collaboration across organizational boundaries, every meeting needs its own compelling purpose, a reason for you and your colleagues to participate.

> Participants in your venture need to know that they can count on meetings to be productive, and worthy of their time and energy.

Many meetings are a waste of time because they are only a rehash of historical information that could easily be distributed in writing. That is not to say that all presentations on historical information are a waste of time. It is largely a matter of priority and expectation. If participants are intending to participate in a review, then so be it. However, most complaints about ineffective meetings are heard when participants are hungry to solve current problems, direct activities, or plan for the future. They are interested to review the past only as it relates to providing insight for the future. They need meetings to be more generative in nature.

Consider your meetings. What percent of time do you spend reporting status and reviewing historical information, versus planning for the future, versus dealing with current issues and opportunities? Whatever your answer, is that the highest and best use of time for both you and your colleagues? Would your answer be different if you could get the right participants in your meetings and you could count on them to prepare in advance, arrive on time and participate fully?

For your venture, to hold participants' attention and interest in your meetings and conference calls, you must find an appropriate balance of:

◆ review of the past
◆ planning for the future
◆ dealing with current issues and opportunities.

**Case study:   Executives learn to focus on one thing at a time** _____
A global, cross-functional executive team in a new high tech company participated in a two-day offsite meeting to plan their future. Subjects included:

- strategic direction for the company
- global organization structure
- effectiveness of this executive team.

As a new team, it was difficult at first for these talented executives to resist the temptation to browse through their calendars, respond to pager messages, rifle through their paperwork or sort their mail while they participated in the discussions. After all, that is what they were used to doing in other meetings in other organizations.

To build trust and confidence among team members, make effective and timely decisions as a group, and ensure a common focus for their efforts, these executives had to agree explicitly to eliminate all distractions and focus on the work at hand. They turned off their cellular phones and pagers. They put their calendars and paperwork in their briefcases and set them aside. And they sat face to face, concentrating on the agenda at hand.

The results were significant:

- The meeting took less time than participants thought it would.
- Critical decisions were made.
- Direction was set based on everyone's input.
- Participants reported feeling refreshed and recharged.

## *Participants*

Should you invite five people to your next meeting or 25? Do you need equal representation from all organizations, or can you count on some to inform and involve others appropriately? Must everyone participate for the entire meeting, or can participants drift in and out? How do you decide whom to include in meetings? The answers to these questions depend on what you want to accomplish, and on what the expectations are of all the individuals and organizations involved. To encourage collaboration across organizational boundaries you want to encourage participation in meetings, yet not waste your colleagues' time. To do so:

- Be clear on your desired outcome – what you want or need to be different as a result of the meeting.
- Clarify the role(s) for each participant – you may need different participants depending on the need for subject matter expertise, decision-making authority, problem resolution, organization of action items and process, quality assurance,

coordination of activities, mediation of conflict, motivation for the group, facilitation, administrative skills, etc.

♦ Itemize the preparation needed by each participant and discern whether and how each participant will be able to comply.

♦ Invite potential participants to help shape the agenda in advance to ensure it is of value to them.

Also, assign someone who is trusted in this role to facilitate key meetings – someone who is trained to:

♦ Clarify objectives and ground rules for the meeting.

♦ Create a 'safe' environment that encourages participation and cooperation.

♦ Manage confusion and conflict among participants.

♦ Maintain the appropriate balance between content and process.

♦ Direct problem solving and brainstorming activities.

♦ Keep the meeting on track.

♦ Ensure closure through review and summary.

♦ Develop action items.

This will enable others involved in the meeting to concentrate on the subject matter, knowing that the meeting process is being managed. In the spirit of collaboration, it also will ensure that:

♦ Strong personalities do not overpower others.

♦ Loud talkers do not dominate soft-spoken participants.

**Case study:   Getting the appropriate people to participate in meetings is worth the risk** _____

In one health care enterprise, organizational boundaries are well established for medical staff, administrators and organized labor. The political climate in this workplace is such that managers pay special attention to titles and positions, and to history of who has attended similar meetings in the past. As a result, many managers have a difficult time deciding on whom to invite to meetings. They rely on old lists to provide guidance. This means that many attendees at meetings add no value. They just take up space in the meeting or waste other participants' time trying to include themselves in the discussion and justify their attendance. In addition, these extraneous participants end up wasting their own time when they could and should have been doing something of real value for the larger enterprise. Many of these meetings are difficult to manage in progress and unproductive by result.

Some managers have decided to be bold – to consider the real purpose of each meeting, and include only those they need to participate based on the desired outcome. In doing so, they have found that discussions are more manageable and focused, everyone participates, and there are actually enough chairs in the room for all attendees. Although some have felt 'left out' of certain discussions, the overall negative impact has been negligible compared to the benefits. _____

## Agenda

As stated before, to encourage collaboration it is always important to be clear about what you are trying to accomplish. Meetings are no different.

> A meeting without a clear agenda is a welcome entry for miscommunication and failure to meet expectations – yours and those of your colleagues.

You must consider both topics and time to be allotted, with respect to the following:

- Is a decision required?
- Do we need to brainstorm innovative ideas?
- Is this to inform the group, only?

If during the meeting you find that you need more time to complete the work required with respect to a particular portion of the agenda, be explicit about asking the group how to proceed. Choices include:

- Stop the current discussion, agreeing to a next step and/or scheduling another meeting to continue the discussion.
- Continue with the topic in progress for a defined amount of time, at which time you will either be finished or have the same choices again.
- Continue with the topic in progress until done, deferring or omitting some other topics and/or extending the allotted time for the meeting.

Even standing meetings such as regular core team meetings should have a high-level agenda template of sorts to help manage expectations for the meeting.

How many meetings have you attended without having an agenda? If you have attended even one meeting without an agenda, that is one too many. To build collaboration across organizational boundaries, be clear on your agenda.

**Case study:   Cross-functional leadership team clarifies agenda** _____

To facilitate better communication and improve productivity across functional boundaries, executives in one company decided to create a template for their weekly leadership team meeting. The agenda was faithfully published three days in advance of the meeting with the following information for each topic:

- ◆ Owner of the topic – the name of the person who submitted the topic and who also would lead that portion of the meeting.
- ◆ Length of time desired for the topic – subject to change if discussion finished before allotted time was used or because the group agreed real time to lengthen the discussion.
- ◆ Desired outcome – (d) decision required, (i) input requested from the group, (u) update, for information only.
- ◆ Importance – ranked 1 (high) to 5 (low) by the executive submitting the item for the agenda.
- ◆ Urgency – ranked 1 (high) to 5 (low), and subject to change by the group at the beginning of the meeting when the agenda was reviewed and prioritized.

The owner of each topic submitted was responsible for necessary background material in advance of each meeting, and all participants were responsible for ensuring that they came to the meetings prepared.

In addition, the agenda allowed room for write-in items at the beginning of the meeting, along with time for the group to prioritize the agenda items. It also included time at the end of each meeting for confirming action items and next steps.

Using this template this leadership team reported accomplishing more during their meetings, and feeling better about working together as a cross-functional team. _____

## Follow up

Even if you hold the best meeting in the world, if you don't follow it up with a record of agreements and action items, you lose. Participants' memories and good intentions fade, and all are easily distracted with other things.

The kind of notes you should publish is dependent on the needs of the group:

♦ Some prefer traditional meeting minutes with a record of what each participant contributed, while others prefer a high-level summary with only agreements and action items included.

♦ Some rely on hardcopy distribution while others prefer to distribute electronically all notes and correspondence for their venture.

Regardless of your group's choice, you need to publish these notes quickly, not waiting several days or weeks to follow up. For maximum impact, and to keep the momentum going, the sooner notes are distributed the better.

**Case study:  'Action items only' minutes are a hit** _____

In one 18-month partnering venture involving representatives from many companies, the core team of ten participants agreed to meet weekly to:

♦ Ensure effective and efficient communication among all involved.

♦ Coordinate activities across company boundaries and among individuals.

♦ Serve as catalysts to enable ongoing progress.

Minutes from these weekly meetings were posted within two hours of the meetings on the venture's Intranet in the form of 'action items only'. All participants were expected to review the minutes faithfully and take special action as needed. Because the group could count on the fact that these notes were published quickly, participants did refer to them as a basis for follow-up.

All were welcome to attend the weekly meetings, but only required to when they had outstanding action items associated with their names. It was up to all participants to keep themselves informed.

Participants in this venture highlighted as key to their success:

♦ an effective core team

♦ appropriate number and types of meetings

♦ 'action items only' minutes from meetings

♦ Intranet technology making information available and accessible to all involved._____

# Monitoring Progress

The only way you will really know if your venture is on track is to monitor progress on an ongoing basis. To do so, you need to agree on:

- Intent – how you measure progress.
- Information – what you track.
- Responsibility – who does the measuring and reporting.
- Reporting – what types, frequencies and formats of reports are prepared.
- Stakeholders – who the audience is for progress reports.
- Review – what kind and frequency of progress review meetings are to be held.
- Consequences – what happens when you meet/exceed/fall short of your plans.

## Measurement tracking systems

Similar to the role of the dashboard in your car, you need to establish and maintain some kind of guidance system for your venture. You need to know whether you are within the speed limit, running low on gas or oil, or about to leave the vehicle with your keys inside. You need information in order to:

- allocate resources
- avoid problems
- celebrate success
- make mid-course corrections.

To facilitate collaboration across organizational boundaries, you and your colleagues need to agree on what kind of system you will use to measure progress toward your objectives. Choices range from formalized computer-based systems offering to capture and report lots of detail, to informal, anecdotal conversations conducted on an *ad hoc* basis. To determine which approach is best for your venture, consider:

- ease of use
- ease of installation and upkeep
- regularity of tracking and reporting
- applicability to all involved in the venture
- level of interest and enthusiasm among participants.

You want to invest in the minimum complexity possible that will give you the most benefit. In other words, keep it simple. Do not overindulge in tracking and reporting lots of details unless you and your colleagues have the time, energy, resources, interest and enthusiasm to keep it going.

Some have found that 'key indicators' or 'dashboard' reports organized according to a format like the one shown in Figure 9 are helpful in monitoring the performance of a cross-organizational collaborative venture. With this technique, using objective and subjective measures, you select, track, summarize and discuss on a regular basis appropriate indicators from a combination of:

- ◆ financial performance
- ◆ customer satisfaction
- ◆ operational performance
- ◆ personal satisfaction.

Others have chosen a 'partnering report card' approach such as the one shown in Figure 10. With this approach parties to the collaboration are asked to evaluate success on a periodic basis. Core team members review and discuss, and set a course to

Concise dashboard reports summarize high-level indicators of performance

| *Financial performance* | *Customer satisfaction* |
|---|---|
| – revenue growth<br>– cost management<br>– margin and profitability<br>– capitalization structure | – marketshare growth<br>– numbers/types of customers<br>– repeat business |
| *Operational performance* | *Personal satisfaction* |
| – schedule achievement<br>– production efficiencies<br>– supply chain excellence<br>– organizational agility | – morale<br>– turnover<br>– learning and development<br>– rewards and recognition |

Fig. 9. Sample dashboard report format.

**Partnering in Action**
**Report card**

| | Score<br>(low) 0 – 100 (high) |
|---|---|
| *Alignment of purpose* – How well aligned are participants around the business context; overall visions and mission; goals and objectives; and priorities for your venture? | |
| *Ability to perform* – How effective are participants at getting the job done; contributing their best; focusing on excellence; making a difference; ensuring individual and shared accountability for outcomes? | |
| *Attention to process* – How effective are meeting management; progress monitoring and reporting; decision-making problem solving; conflict resolution; governance; and internal/external measurement systems for your venture? | |
| *Acuity of communication* – How well does your group exhibit openness/candor; use discipline and skill to provide and receive information; and ensure timely and accurate feedback in all aspects of your venture? | |
| *Attitude of mutual trust and respect* – How well does your group share risk and reward; blend autonomy and interdependence; acknowledge and support each other? | |
| *Adaptability to learn and change* – How much attention is paid to continuous learning for all individuals; after action briefings; institutional memory; continuous improvement? | |
| Total score (0 – 600) | |

© The Bellwood Group

Fig. 10. Parnering in Action report card.

improve, period by period. Still others prefer to meet and discuss, either formally or informally. In doing so they:

- review business context
- present current status

◆ coordinate activities
◆ check for alignment
◆ clarify action items and next steps.

Whatever you use internally within the venture, ensure that your measurements are aligned with how external evaluators will keep score. These external evaluators may include shareholders, customers, anyone who has an interest in the success of your venture.

### Case study: Cross-functional hospitality management team measures the 'vital few'

In one hospitality organization, the cross-functional management team comprising leaders from housekeeping, reservations, front desk, food services, facility operations and maintenance, gift shop and concierge services developed a Customer Service Scorecard like the one shown in Figure 11 to help them stay focused on what is important to their guests. They chose to focus on items that required the entire team's participation, and that could be evaluated by staff, managers and guests alike.

All staff members are invited to fill out scorecards weekly. Guests are invited to submit comments at any time during their stay. Results are consolidated and reported weekly for discussion by the cross-functional management team. As action plans are commissioned, progress is also monitored. _____

| Customer Service Scorecard | | |
|---|---|---|
| *Criteria* | *Rating*<br>1 (low) – 5 (high)<br>NA = not applicable | *Comments* |
| Clean facilities | 1 2 3 4 5 NA | |
| Hassle-free experience | 1 2 3 4 5 NA | |
| Friendly staff | 1 2 3 4 5 NA | |
| Problem-solvers | 1 2 3 4 5 NA | |
| Breakfast served on time | 1 2 3 4 5 NA | |
| Other – please identify | 1 2 3 4 5 NA | |

Fig. 11. Sample Customer Service Scorecard.

### Recovery mechanism

When things go wrong – and they will – what will you do about them? How will you hold each other accountable for the desired collaborative behaviors? What are the consequences of not living up to your commitments regarding collaborative behavior? If your answer is that there are no consequences, will those involved in your venture behave collaboratively? They may if they are used to doing so, or have experienced personal benefit by doing so in the past. But if they have not been part of other successful collaborative ventures, it is more likely that they will revert to their old (and previously successful) behaviors – whatever they are.

To encourage collaborative behavior you must put in place a 'recovery mechanism' to minimize the impact of mistakes, lapses and/or regression. You must *plan in advance* what will be done when participants do not behave in a collaborative way. Specifically:

- Accountability and authority to redirect the process when something goes astray must be clear. In the most powerful collaborative ventures such accountability and authority belong to everyone in the group. It is expected that each participant will speak up and take action – in an appropriate way – when something in the process is not right.
- Consequences of offending behavior must be understood. For example, will coaching be available to those who mis-step, or will those individuals be removed from the venture? You should not assume that things will fix themselves.

**Case study:   CEO requests 'lapse mechanism'** _____

As he was trying to develop more cross-functional collaboration across the marketing, sales, finance, service and development functions of his company, one CEO determined that a 'lapse mechanism' was key to the group's success. He knew that individuals would fall prey to old behaviors even after making agreements for how things would work moving forward.

A leadership team with representatives from all functions was formed to manage these 'lapses' on a temporary basis. For six months this team met on a weekly basis to review collaborative successes during the past week and redirect behavior if needed for the coming week. The agenda was explicit – examine how the company does its work: the process, not the content. All experiences, regardless how big or small, were appropriate subjects for this team. The objective was to transform individuals' daily work into a more collaborative experience. Hence the team had to deal with whatever made up daily work.

For those circumstances where collaboration did not meet participants' expectations, individuals were coached on how to work more effectively with colleagues next time.

What worked for this company included:

- ◆ clarity of vision regarding the desired outcome
- ◆ specific focus to monitor success and resolve issues quickly
- ◆ proactive coaching for individuals._____

## Making and Keeping to Decisions

Many collaborative ventures get bogged down due to ineffective decision-making. Beyond whether the actual content of decisions is good or bad, complaints include:

- ◆ lack of accountability for decisions
- ◆ slow decision process
- ◆ decisions made at the wrong level
- ◆ inconsistent approach to decision-making
- ◆ lack of communication about decisions
- ◆ undermining or sabotaging decisions.

There are lots of reasons why such problems with decision-making exist, including:

- ◆ distrust
- ◆ fear
- ◆ unclear roles and responsibilities
- ◆ incompetence
- ◆ old habits
- ◆ loss of confidence
- ◆ inadequate communication tools
- ◆ lack of commitment.

Decision-making for your venture doesn't have to be like that. You can create a positive environment, where individuals and organizations are counted on to make, communicate and support decisions on an ongoing basis. To do so:

- ◆ Clarify each participant's role, responsibility, authority and accountability with respect to decision-making.

- ◆ Remove organizational obstacles such at title, seniority, or even 'in boxes' that only serve to delay decisions.
- ◆ Ensure that those involved are confident and comfortable to make the kinds of decisions they need to make, and to manage the decision-making process, by providing coaching and mentoring as needed.
- ◆ Agree on guiding principles for decision-making such as:
  - – decisions are made at the lowest level appropriate, by those impacted
  - – all decisions are aligned with the core values and visions for the venture
  - – all stakeholders are informed in advance of decisions in process
  - – consensus process is used to make decisions; those who disagree are heard, but must support or depart if the group makes the decision to move ahead
- ◆ Establish clear communication strategy so that decisions can be communicated easily to all who need to know.
- ◆ Instill a spirit of learning among those involved in your venture so that all can continue to improve both the decision-making process and the quality of decisions being made.

**Case study:   Decisions about decision-making can be difficult to make** __

In one high tech venture involving two companies, decisions throughout the venture were becoming increasingly slow in an increasingly competitive market. This venture was losing market share and missing windows of opportunity.

Executives from the two companies had to face the fact that they had created an enterprise with:

- ◆ too many levels of management
- ◆ hierarchical orientation
- ◆ too many people involved in every detail
- ◆ no accountability for decisions
- ◆ no consequences
- ◆ risk-averse behavior
- ◆ poor communication.

To improve the situation, they focused on:

- ◆ Developing a clear picture of the desired decision-making process.

- Clarifying individuals' roles, responsibilities and accountabilities in the decision-making process.
- Changing their personal behavior to not be involved in every detail and to support others' decisions.
- Recognizing and rewarding those who made effective decisions and communicated them to others.

It was not easy. Some old habits proved difficult to change. The change had to be managed carefully and with compassion. And, as with any change, some moved forward quickly while others lagged behind, holding on to previous ways of doing things. _____

## Solving Problems and Resolving Conflicts

This is an area where you really get to practice what you preach. Your willingness and commitment to deal collaboratively with problems and conflicts goes a long way toward building collaboration across organizational boundaries. The key is to:
- Agree up front, before you experience any problems or conflicts, what the process will be for handling them.
- Invoke necessary tools and techniques early to help minimize the number and types of problems and conflicts you experience throughout your venture.

Two types of problems or conflicts can arise in your collaborative venture:
- **Task-related** – those that happen because someone has made a mistake; participants differ with respect to goals, objectives or priorities; or participants have a disagreement about a specific topic under consideration.
- **Relationship-related** – those that exist because of how participants are relating with each other.

In his work on Relationship Awareness Theory (reference 'Strength Deployment Inventory.'(R)), Dr. Elias H. Porter defined two types of conflicts, both related to individuals' motivational value systems:
- **Warranted conflict** – conflict that occurs when those involved do not agree on the desired outcome; sincere disagreement about the goal.
- **Unwarranted conflict** – conflict that occurs when those involved agree on the goal but disagree on the approach to

achieving the goal; frequently the result of people's behavior being misunderstood or misinterpreted.

Dr Porter's work asserts that in the face of conflict and opposition you and your colleagues can be expected to be predictably variable in deploying your personal strengths. The speed and intensity with which you and your colleagues progress through three stages of conflict management varies. It depends on many variables, including:

+ How much each individual values the relationship.
+ The degree of danger each participant perceives.
+ The amount of power held by each individual involved.
+ How close the issue is to each person's core values.

Understanding the problem is half the battle – whether the issue is task-related or relationship-related; whether the conflict is warranted or unwarranted; and how each person involved perceives the situation. Just like a physician trying to diagnose and treat a patient's illness, you must clarify the real problem in order to help solve it. If you don't, you will likely treat only the symptoms. And just like with an illness, by treating only the symptoms you run the risk of surfacing more and different symptoms, and/or actually making the situation worse.

## Problem management mechanism

To minimize the negative impacts of problems and conflicts, regardless of whether they are task or relationship-related, you need a mechanism for your venture that enables participants to:

+ Identify problems and conflicts as they arise.
+ Notify others that a problem or conflict exists.
+ Classify a problem or conflict according to its importance and urgency.
+ Escalate situations according to importance and urgency.
+ Manage resolution for a problem or conflict.

Many choices exist for handling task-related problems. These include:

+ Problem management software systems.
+ 'Help desk' or 'hot line' arrangements where participants can

call to report a problem and seek help.
- Meetings with an agenda dedicated to problem management.
- Creative problem-solving work sessions.

Resolving relationship-related problems and conflicts often requires some additional care:
- coaching
- facilitated work sessions
- mediation
- management intervention.

You need to be able to recognize when the conflict is getting in the way of getting work done. When these situations arise you must deal with them quickly and carefully, otherwise they are likely to get worse.

### Case study: Health care executives convene to determine how to resolve conflicts

Nine executives who have to collaborate across functional, organizational and geographic boundaries convened what they called a Management Retreat to figure out how to resolve conflicts. The objectives for their one-day work session were as follows:
- Create a toolbox for conflict resolution.
- Build skills to resolve conflicts in a variety of situations.
- Develop a process to guide conflict resolution.
- Establish a way to resolve conflict openly.
- Learn to deal productively with existing issues that keep us from achieving our goals.
- Develop trust among this team.
- Set the stage for operationalizing our knowledge.
- Gain commitment to next steps.

Their discussion and discovery included:
- Clarification of why conflict resolution is important to the collaboration – for example, both real and perceived issues were keeping the group from achieving its goals; participants were lacking in skills, experience and confidence regarding how to deal with difficult situations.
- Reaffirmation of a basis for working together to resolve conflicts – specifics of

how each participant values the contributions of the others; the foundation for conflict resolution.

♦ Identification of causes for conflict among the team – these included:

– ineffective interpersonal behavior
disrespect
refusal to work together
negative comments
seemingly deliberate efforts to confuse
defensiveness

– lack of communication/different points of view
blaming others
no follow-up
not taking time to communicate
rehashing the past
promoting self over team
not listening
failure to confront negative messages/behavior allows conflict to build up
actions and/or style are interpreted incorrectly

– inadequate information sharing
either not sharing or actively withholding important information from teammates
distorting information to evoke controversy
two-faced – saying one thing and doing another

– conflicting demands on time, loyalty, energy
need to be nice but desire to not be nice
individual objectives appear more important that group goals
not valuing differences of opinion
wasting time and resources

- breech of integrity
failure to maintain integrity of agreements by subsequent actions.

♦ Tools and commitments for conflict resolution – as summarized by their five-step prescription to stop keeping issues in the background and to get them on the table to be dealt with:

1 Think about and own up to how you might be contributing to the problem.
2 Organize your thoughts and approach to confronting the situation.
3 Take the risk and raise the issue with the following guidelines:

– choose from among (a) one-on-one or (b) with this group as part of our agenda and/or (3) with help from a facilitator
– remember to remain present during the discussion(s), be a generous listener, and do not be defensive.

4 Reach understanding of the issue, and agree a plan of action including how to follow up and evaluate.

5 Evaluate and applaud success._____

## Preventative measures

A better choice is for you to do more work up front to avoid problems and conflicts. Many of the task-related problems and conflicts that you and your colleagues might experience can be avoided by creating alignment among all parties up front. You need to ensure that all agree on what you are trying to accomplish together and how you will get the job done.

Most relationship-related problems and conflicts are avoidable, too. You and your colleagues can define how you are going to work together. You can:

♦ Clarify up front what behavior is acceptable, and what is not – in as much detail as participants need in order to get the message.

♦ Ensure that all know how to behave according to plan – train and coach participants, where necessary.

♦ Align rewards for your venture to reward the desired collaborative behavior.

To minimize the number and types of problems and conflicts for your venture:

♦ Create as much alignment as possible among participants – alignment regarding what your venture is all about, how you all will work together, what you should expect from each other, all the topics of this book.

♦ Ensure that all participants are competent – function, form and fit as described in Chapter 3.

♦ Develop understanding and appreciation among participants of who these individuals are at core – their personality types, their frames of reference, their relating styles, etc. The more you and your colleagues genuinely understand and value each other, the fewer difficulties you will have in getting along with each other.

**Case study:   Rocks in the Road Work Sessions clear pathway for success** _____

In one collaborative venture core team members decided to be proactive. They convened what they called Rocks in the Road Work Sessions on a monthly basis. Their objective was to identify and mitigate in advance issues that might have a negative impact on their work. They developed the following standard agenda for these monthly meetings:

◆ Brainstorm list of potential 'rocks' that they might have to face.
◆ Sort, sift, and prioritize potential rocks as to urgency, importance and likely impact if nothing is done.
◆ Identify ways to alleviate or minimize impact.
◆ Discuss bigger picture to understand how to avoid similar issues in the future.
◆ Confirm action items and next steps.

This technique was straightforward, but non-trivial. It took everyone's participation. Everyone had to be forward looking. They were counted on to come to the table with prospective issues. Everyone had to be open and honest about potential difficulties on the horizon. Everyone's contribution was important in generating solutions together.

These Rocks in the Road Work Sessions allowed this group to stay focused on the important issues, and to meet their objectives with the least amount of trauma and drama._____

## Key Tools and Techniques

Key processes will dictate how your venture operates. To maximize collaboration across organizational boundaries, gain agreement up front regarding your choice of governance. In particular:

✔ Ensure that everyone's time is used wisely through effective meeting management techniques.
✔ Enable decision-making at appropriate levels throughout the venture – with accountability for making, communicating, and supporting decisions vested in all participants.
✔ Minimize the negative impacts of problems and conflicts by creating alignment and understanding up front, and by incorporating proactive mechanisms to deal with problems

and conflicts as they arise.

✔ Help everyone stay focused on objectives and priorities by maintaining visibility on milestones, and by monitoring and managing progress on an ongoing basis.

✔ Manage your relationships with your colleagues so that they are positive and productive.

CHAPTER 5

# Acuity of Communication

C ommunication is repeatedly cited as either an enabler or a block in collaborating successfully across organizational boundaries. Lack of communication is often blamed for

*   missed schedules
*   over-run budgets
*   broken trust
*   inadequate results.

To build successful business partnering relationships across organizational boundaries you must do your part to ensure successful communication. Put simply, you must ensure that over and over again, throughout the life of your venture:

*   the **right message** gets broadcast
*   in the **right way**
*   to the **right people**
*   with the **right result**.

A lot is written about communication. Many publications exist on how to be a better speaker, how to give presentations, tips for business writing, how to listen, etc. There also are many seminars and workshops for improving communication.

The intention here is not to duplicate what already exists, but rather to call your attention to some fundamentals that make the difference in successful business partnering relationships and to make suggestions for creating real acuity of communication in your venture.

Those who complain about communication being inadequate in 'would be' collaborative ventures cite one or more of the following as culprits:

*   Not knowing what is going on.
*   Not being included in decision-making.
*   Not understanding why things are being done a certain way.

- Lack of follow through from words to action.
- Too much 'data' and not enough 'information'.
- Inadequate coordination of activities among individuals and organizations.
- Unreconciled differences of opinion.
- Too much time wasted in meetings.
- Ineffective communication (approaches) by others.

Those who praise communication as an important enabler of collaboration across organizational boundaries repeatedly highlight the following ingredients as key to their success:

- The **personal effectiveness of individuals** in communicating with others.
- An effective **process for managing time together** in meetings and work sessions.
- An **accessible central repository** housing all important information relevant to the venture.

We all can learn something from those who have done things right.

## Ensuring Your Own Basic Skills

To ensure successful collaboration across organizational boundaries, you personally must be an effective communicator – both providing and receiving information.

A variety of different things can get in your way to keep you from being an effective communicator. These include:

- Real barriers such as native languages, time zone differences, industry or organizational jargon.
- Your own ability to read, write, speak and hear.
- Your personal commitment and dedication to making your communication effective and efficient.
- Your proficiency with communication tools such as voice mail, email and other specialized technology-based systems.

Even so, no excuses on this one.

> You should not be part of the problem. Make it your business to be a 'good' communicator.

If communication is to support rather than impede your collaborative venture, you must do your part. For example:

- ◆ If you need to learn how to write better business correspondence, do so.
- ◆ If you don't understand what your colleague just told you, ask for clarification.
- ◆ If you need to get some help to prepare and deliver better presentations, go to a class or work with a coach or colleague who does this well.
- ◆ If real barriers exist, remove them. For example, make yourself available for that conference call after hours; get an interpreter to help with language differences; learn the jargon for your venture.
- ◆ If you are not very good at listening to others, change that.
- ◆ If you find yourself hesitating to send an email message or find the document you need from the computer because you are intimidated by technology, turn that around. Learn how to use the appropriate technology.
- ◆ If others are confused by your messages, clarify your objectives, content and format.

**Case study:   Sometimes, less is more** _____

Jack, a financial manager involved in a worldwide venture, has a habit of talking too much. Regularly, when a simple 'yes' or 'no' will suffice during meetings and conference calls, he embarks on lengthy, and many times irrelevant descriptions, prescriptions, examples and excuses. In addition, he likes to have the last word in any conversation. As a result, instead of being perceived by his colleagues as a value-added team member, he is regarded as an 'irritant', 'detriment', 'necessary evil' and someone to be avoided if at all possible.

In contrast Mary, an operations manager involved in the same venture, is known to listen to others, ask questions when clarification is needed, and make her points succinctly with appropriate supporting information. She is respected by her colleagues around the world, and a 'welcome participant' in meetings and conference calls. _____

# Knowing Your Colleagues

Once you have your own house in order you must focus on the others in your venture. Not to change them, but to understand who they are. To put it selfishly, you need to know how to get others to receive your messages in the way that you intend. Otherwise, you lose.

You must do your whole job of communicating. In all your efforts to communicate with others it is your responsibility to:

♦ Communicate in such a way that you are understood by your colleagues.

♦ Get feedback that your message is received and understood.

## *Using the right 'language'*

To build collaboration across organizational boundaries, do not assume that others understand and speak your language. Just like visiting different countries, unless or until you and your colleagues have agreed on one language for your venture, you must use as many languages as it takes to communicate with your colleagues; 'language' in this case refers to more than native tongue.

You may need to provide engineers with models, drawings, or other specification information to understand your point. Accountants in your venture might be better served with facts and figures in spreadsheet format. You may need to use different vocabulary with marketers than will be effective with technicians. Sales people may need to understand features and benefits while operations people might prefer to know about how your idea will work. Executives might prefer to receive a high-level summary from you while others may need details to understand your message and support what you are trying to do. You may need to draw pictures for some, provide narrative description for others, allow others to taste, smell or touch what you are trying to express. All these differences might be magnified as you cross organizational boundaries.

Your colleagues may not tell you directly what they need or want to be able to understand your contributions. It is up to you to understand them.

**Case study:   All 'yes's are not alike** _____

In one high tech collaboration involving engineers from both a Japanese and an American company, participants had to learn the meaning of the word 'yes'. In the early stages of the venture, the American participants took a 'yes' response from their Japanese counterparts as 'I agree with you and will proceed as you request.' At the same time, the Japanese participants used the word 'yes' to mean only 'I hear you' or 'I understand what you are saying.'

Pleased with their work sessions and conference calls, and making assumptions about what would happen next, the American engineers were repeatedly disappointed when what they thought had been agreed to was not carried out. Their Japanese counterparts did not understand the disappointment because they did not think they had agreed to proceed.

To eliminate the unwarranted disappointment and ensure more effective communication, these engineers had to learn to:

◆ ask more specific questions

◆ answer questions with more than just 'yes' or 'no'

◆ confirm specific agreements at the end of each encounter._____

# Connecting with Others

> Your communication in a collaborative venture is worthwhile only if you connect with your colleagues.

Talking 'at' your colleagues offers no benefit for your venture. Writing documents that are not used does no good. Both waste your time. You must speak so that your colleagues will listen. You must write so that they will read. You must motivate them to want your contribution. You can do this by connecting with them – meeting them where they are and making your communication relevant for them. Yes, they should do the same for you, but until they do you must manage the connection.

You can ensure that you connect with your colleagues in a variety of ways. For example:

◆ Become personally acquainted with your colleagues so that you really know them and so that you can use words, pictures, analogies, etc that mean something to them and that evoke the response you want.

◆ Use personality-profiling tools such as the Myers-Briggs Type Indicator® with all key participants in your venture to identify distinguishing characteristics related to communication.

♦ Have a conversation with your colleagues individually or as a group about how best to connect with them.

♦ Learn to appeal to all the senses – sight, hearing, taste, smell and touch – as you communicate with others. This technique is especially helpful for large and/or geographically dispersed groups where connecting with each unique individual is not practical.

Please take the time to consider how well you connect with your colleagues, and note what steps you might take to improve in this area.

**Case study:   Knowing colleagues' preferences makes it easier to connect** _____

In one collaborative business venture involving 12 senior managers in six geographic locations around the world, the group met face-to-face to determine how to communicate effectively and efficiently across time zones and language barriers.

First they learned about each other's communication preferences, as summarized in Figure 12.

Second they observed several things about the group, including:

♦ They had a potential problem in that nine people involved in the venture preferred talking as the way of providing information to others but only four people preferred listening as the way of receiving information from others.

♦ They understood why Ms Akimoto, Ms Jones, Ms Heibert and Mr Smith (who preferred talking and listening) seemed to communicate well with each other but not as well with the rest of the group.

♦ With several native languages in the group, they thought having things in writing probably made it easier for many to understand.

As a result, they all agreed to modify their personal behavior to:

♦ Provide written information up front for important discussions and decisions to be made.

♦ Follow informal conversations with written summary of agreements.

♦ Expect that all would not have read and understood material provided in advance of a meeting.

♦ Touch base personally with those who prefer to listen._____

| Preference in *receiving* information from others | Preference in *providing* information to others |
|---|---|
| Read | Write |
| Ms Bell   Ms Chen<br>Mr Davis         Mr O'Malley<br>Mr Sullivan   Mr Tran<br>Mr Walsh        Mr Wong | Ms Chen   Mr Smith<br><br>Mr Wong |
| Listen | Talk |
| Ms Akimoto<br><br>Ms Heibert<br>Ms Jones        Mr Smith | Ms Akimoto   Ms Bell<br>Mr Davis         Ms Heibert<br>Ms Jones   Mr O'Malley<br>Mr Sullivan         Mr Tran<br>Mr Walsh |

Fig. 12.   Example of communication preferences.

## Clarifying the Objective

To be effective in communicating with others, you need to be clear regarding your objective – what you want to happen as a result of your message. When your intent is clear it is easier for your colleagues to meet your expectations. Put another way, eliminating any guesswork on the part of your colleagues improves both the communication and the outcome. Eliminating guesswork improves collaboration.

With each message you provide to your colleagues, whether verbally or in writing, clarify your objective. If you are just informing your colleagues, say so. If you are intending to teach or guide them, make your purpose explicit. If you are commanding them, there should be no doubt. If you want a response, make a specific request.

Please consider how you should achieve your objective.

> To build collaboration across organizational boundaries, your communication needs to build up, not to tear down.

Even when you need to criticize someone's work, you must choose your communication wisely. Your words, timing, format, tone, body language, place, sense of urgency, who else you inform and involve – the entire package containing your message must be positioned so that your colleagues get the right message. Considering that it is hard enough for most of us to communicate effectively when things are going well, you must take extra care when you are faced with a difficult or stressful situation:

◆  Harness your own motivation to ensure that it is positive and productive.

◆  Remove extraneous junk from your message.

◆  Separate fact from feeling.

◆  Use appropriate means and mechanisms to get your message across.

To check yourself on this point, consider what some others have found to be helpful – ask 'What would be lost if I do not communicate this in this way?'

### Case study:   Poor communication yields frustration and embarrassment

Jim, an executive in a high tech company and participant in a joint venture involving three companies, lamented a recent situation where his own lack of clarity resulted in:

◆  frustration with a subordinate

◆  embarrassment in front of his colleagues and his boss.

Jim had asked Debbie, a subordinate manager in his organization, to prepare a report for discussion in an important meeting involving his boss and key representatives from the other two companies involved. The report arrived in time for the meeting, but in a different form from what he had envisioned. In addition, he entered the meeting with questions about the data, and unsure whether or not the conclusions presented in the report were appropriate. The meeting was uncomfortable for everyone involved:

◆  important questions were not answered

◆  Jim and Debbie did not behave like a team in front of the others

◆  Debbie felt unappreciated

◆  Jim's boss and colleagues were left unsatisfied

◆  other team members lost confidence in Jim and Debbie.

As he recounted this unhappy experience, Jim admitted that he had left his subordinate to her own devices to create her vision of the report. He had not given Debbie any guidelines for the report format, and he had not established explicit plans to review the report's content and format before the meeting. In addition, it was only when he saw the report moments before the meeting that he formed a true picture of how the report should look, what specific data it should contain and what conclusions it should represent.

If Jim had spent adequate time with Debbie to clarify his expectations and agree what needed to be accomplished both with the report and in the meeting, this communication could have been more effective. _____

# Seeking to Understand

When you receive something from a colleague – whether written, verbal, or three-dimensional – make it your business to understand. For example:

- Understand the entire message – its context, content and format.
- Resist the urge to guess – ask for clarification where you need to.
- Test your assumptions – be conscious of any filters you are using to receive the message, including your biases, prejudices, past experiences, etc.

**Case study:   Collaborators agree on guidelines to improve communication**  _____

In one multi-disciplinary service organization covering all of the United States, the leadership team needed to devise a way to communicate effectively in order to focus attention quickly and accurately, and make collaborative decisions. To make it easier for their colleagues to understand what they wanted to convey, they agreed on the following guidelines for presenting proposals for action:

Documentation – in the form of email, Word document and/or PowerPoint presentation – should accompany discussion of good ideas wanting approval when any of the following conditions exist:
- The idea has *potential to touch more than one function and/or location.*
- The proposal represents *a change in how we do things.*
- Moving forward in the proposed way would have *major impact on overall goals.*

The objective of your documentation is to make it easy for someone else to 'sell' the idea on your behalf.

Always include the following in your thinking, conversations, presentations and proposal documents:

◆ *Context and background* – what is the business issue or opportunity being addressed by this, and why now?
  – consider the 'big picture'
  – maintain perspective – consider your situation in relation to others.
◆ *Scope of the proposal* – what is the recommendation and why
  – clearly articulate the goal
  – statement of strategy.
◆ *Key assumptions* – clearly state all assumptions you are making.
◆ *Alternative solutions* – what has been examined and why, along with a comparative analysis, for example, pro/con analysis or key 'differentiators' among the choices; including the 'do nothing' case.
  – specific trade-offs and/or implications.
◆ *Cost/benefit analysis* – *pro forma* of investment and expected return, including timing of both dollars and other resources as well as expected benefits.
  – budget requirements
  – ROI (return on investment) analysis
  – statement of value/specific benefits
  – specific scenarios – if/then/what if.
◆ *Risk analysis* – what do we have to be mindful of if we proceed?
  – What are the risks and proposed mitigation plans?
◆ *Recommended next step(s)* – including timeline and review process.

Remember too that:
◆ All information must be *accurate*.
◆ Level of *detail must be appropriate* for your audience.
◆ *You want to be concise* in your discussions and documented proposals – more information is not necessarily better.
◆ You should *anticipate others' questions* and be ready with your answers.
◆ *Timing* for your proposal is important – it must be appropriate in relation to all the other things going on.
◆ You must *develop buy-in* among 'affected' parties – including those who will be impacted by your proposal, those who can influence whether it succeeds or not, and those whose support/approval you need in order to move forward.
◆ You must demonstrate evidence of *good business judgment*.
◆ When in doubt you should *test your assumptions* with others before you build your case._____

## Keeping Communication Flowing

> Don't wait for an SOS to send or receive a message.

Without communication there is no collaboration. It's the nature of the beast – by its very nature collaboration means 'together', 'with others'. More so than just 'doing your job', in a collaborative venture you should expect to:

- Participate in more meetings and work sessions.
- Initiate and receive more telephone calls, video conferences and email messages.
- Generate and review more documentation.
- Spend more time doing things to coordinate and cooperate with others.

It is imperative that you focus on keeping communication channels open among all individuals and organizations involved in your collaborative venture. You need communication for your venture to be easy, so that all will participate. This means that you must break down any and all barriers to communication, whether they are real or perceived.

Also, although this may seem counter intuitive, the more dynamic the situation, the more you need to communicate with others. Make sure that all participants stay 'on the same page' regarding assumptions and expectations. New information, changes to requirements, fast developing progress, unforeseen problems, all are reasons for you to confer with colleagues. If you don't, it is likely that they will proceed with old information, assumptions, and expectations, and that together you will end up with wasted effort, rework, bad feelings, missed deadlines and/or cost overruns.

If done well, these meetings, phone conversations, video conferences, email messages and other documentation should yield a greater result than you can accomplish without them. Your challenge is to do these things well.

To make the most of all of your interactions with others:

- Clarify the objective for each interaction – specifically what you want to accomplish with each and every meeting or conference call, and how you will recognize success.

- Include those who need to be involved in the interaction and be clear as to why they need to be involved – clarify expectations regarding their input, decision-making authority, personal learning, etc so that you do not waste your time or theirs.
- Provide necessary background and context to others – *necessary* information, not miscellaneous data, and with enough lead time to allow appropriate preparation on their parts.
- Come prepared for the interaction – do your homework by reviewing appropriate material in advance, making notes, completing action items from prior interactions, etc.
- Manage the process of the interaction – ensure that others understand the objective, background and context and their role in the interaction.
- Gain agreement on action items and next steps – do not assume that others have come to the same conclusions that you have.
- Follow up on the interaction – a record of agreements, a 'tickler' to remind others, whatever it takes for those in your venture to be successful.

Also, you need to remain conscious of how communication is going among participants in your venture. For example:
- When someone talks, does everyone listen?
- Are appropriate individuals and organizations involved in conversations, correspondence, meetings and the decision-making process?
- Are you dealing effectively with time zones?
- How are you handling language translation(s) if needed?
- Beyond native tongue, is the jargon for your venture common to all involved?
- How well are your feedback loops working so that you know messages have been received and understood?
- To what degree is communication among participants easy, relaxed and natural?
- How skilled are you and your colleagues at reading people to know when feelings are hurt, unspoken concerns or issues exist, communication is not effective?

- ◆ How versatile are you and your colleagues in communicating in different ways in order to improve overall communication among individuals and organizations involved in your venture?
- ◆ If you or one of your colleagues realizes that communication is not what it should be, what happens?

If something pertaining to communication is not working, fix it. Do whatever it takes to ensure a smooth and steady flow of communication among all individuals and organizations involved in your venture.

### Case study:   Feedback via anonymous written scorecard is replaced with dialogue_____

Principals in one venture learned the hard way how to give and receive feedback in a way that promoted learning and maintained collaborative relationships. At first they attempted to provide feedback in the form of monthly written scorecards. They agreed on a template for items to be included on the card, a numeric scoring scheme to be used, and a process as follows:

- ◆ key participants complete the scorecard on a monthly basis
- ◆ results are tallied by an administrator
- ◆ scorecard summaries are distributed to core team members from each company.

This technique worked marginally well when scores were good. At least then the cards did no harm to relationships. Participants could review their cards and set them aside, having received a small token of validation that all was well.

However, if feedback was less than excellent, these scorecards created major problems for the group. Numbers on the cards pierced individuals' feelings like arrows. Egos were bruised, feelings were hurt, communication was thwarted, and trust was broken. Organizations moved to protect and defend their own perspectives and actions, over those of the group. Without the benefit of specific examples and opportunity for explanation and discussion regarding specific situations, collaboration declined.

After just a couple of months of this discomfort, core team members agreed to use the scorecard only as a basis for discussion. They learned to have regular conversations about the issues, concentrating on what needed to be improved rather than who was wrong. Additionally they learned, even in tough times, to treat each other in a productive and positive manner. _____

# Incorporating Self-service

So far, everything included in this chapter has to do with **push** forms of communication – things that you push out to others or that are pushed onto you. You also can derive benefit within your venture by means of **pull** communication – putting the responsibility on you and your colleagues as individuals to pull what you need.

You do this already as you ask questions of your colleagues or search the library or Internet to research a subject in general or get the latest updated information. You 'pull' what you need. The opportunity is to institutionalize this act so that you and your colleagues 'pull' what you need on an ongoing basis, from a repository that can be trusted to meet your needs.

With the evolution of technology, you have the opportunity to be proactive in establishing and maintaining systems to encourage more 'self-service' communication. You can establish a 'home base' for key information pertaining to your venture:

+ text documents and reports
+ engineering drawings
+ spreadsheets
+ photographs
+ budgets and financial reports
+ project management information
+ news clips
+ presentation materials
+ correspondence
+ video clips
+ email messages
+ meeting minutes.

By creating one 'home base' for all information, you can place the responsibility and accountability for keeping others involved and informed, and being informed, on all participants. You also get an institutional memory from which to learn and grow (covered more in Chapter 7).

Necessary technology tools include:

+ personal computers
+ network interface hardware and software
+ Internet or Intranet interface hardware and software

- data base systems software
- portal technology
- search engine software
- security systems.

Additionally, you must establish some scheme and discipline among the team concerning when, why, and how to label, file, and manage various types of information – for example:

- What kind of information should be included?
- Who has rights to access and/or update the information?
- How should information be labeled and filed so that others can find it?
- How will outdated information be handled?

**Case study:   Personal preparation makes the difference** _____

John and Sam are two executives involved in a worldwide collaborative venture involving four companies. They are on the same distribution lists for memos and emails. They attend many of the same meetings. Sam repeatedly spouts phrases such as 'nobody told me', and 'I didn't know'. He shows up at meetings without the requisite background information, and frequently without any means for making notes.

At the same time, John arrives at meetings with requisite material in hand, yellow highlighter pen markings frequently visible on the printed material and small notes in the margins. He pulls what he needs from the central repository of information. This visible evidence of preparation makes quite an impression on his colleagues. When John speaks, his colleagues listen. _____

## Key Tools and Techniques

Effective communication is required for successful collaboration across organizational boundaries. To improve the effectiveness of communication for your venture:

- ✔ Know your team mates and their communication needs and preferences relative to your venture.
- ✔ Gain agreement on expectations regarding communication for your venture – for example type, frequency, format, methods, response times, etc.
- ✔ Distinguish between and use both 'push' and 'pull' communication as appropriate.

✔ Build a useful information repository for your venture – one that is organized for easy storage and retrieval of information by those involved.

✔ Make your personal communication effective – be clear on what you want from each communication with others, and use tools and techniques to your advantage.

✔ Periodically examine and enhance the effectiveness of communication in your venture.

# CHAPTER 6

# Attitude of Mutual Trust and Respect

> *The level of collaboration is directly proportional to the level of trust and respect among all parties involved.*

Although the words 'trust' and 'respect' by themselves might have different meanings, often these two words are lumped together by those describing the tone, feeling or attitude of their collaborative ventures. They use these words to describe whether and how they feel valued and appreciated and how they feel about working with their colleagues. For example:

+ 'We all trust and respect each other.'
+ 'I don't trust him.'
+ 'They don't treat me with respect.'

Building mutual trust and respect among participants in a collaborative venture:

+ enhances productivity by focusing attention on the work
+ encourages both individual and group innovation
+ minimizes costs for monitoring
+ maximizes individual and group energy and enthusiasm for the venture.

Conversely, lack of trust and respect in a collaborative venture:

+ diverts attention
+ stifles innovation
+ increases costs
+ drains energy.

Whether trust and respect are warranted is not the subject of this writing. Rather, the focus of this chapter is to:

+ Remind you that some amounts of trust and respect are required for successful collaboration across organizational boundaries.
+ Offer you some insights regarding what it takes to build trust and respect among participants in a business partnering relationship so that the work will be successful.

Some groups prefer to focus explicitly on building trust and respect as part of setting ground rules for partnering. Others prefer to deal implicitly with trust and respect among participants – allowing trust and respect to evolve naturally as they work together. Both approaches are effective, based on participants' preferences.

## Securing a Basis for Trust and Respect

Common causes of distrust or lack of respect in a collaborative venture include:

- incompetence or the presumption of incompetence
- inappropriate interpersonal behavior
- hidden agendas or perception of hidden agendas
- misalignment of rewards and recognition
- untrustworthy information
- inadequate systems and processes
- individual breech of integrity.

The prescription then is straightforward, albeit important. To build trust and respect among participants you must ensure that:

- Participants are competent to perform the work at hand.
- Interpersonal behavior and communication skills are acceptable.
- A common purpose exists for the venture.
- Measurements, recognition and rewards are aligned with desired outcomes.
- Information throughout the venture is trustworthy.
- Systems and processes are appropriate in scope and form.
- All participants remain in integrity.

As this list highlights, the ingredients for successful collaboration across organizational boundaries are interrelated. For example, as you build competence, interpersonal skills, and the ability to perform (Chapter 3), you increase the level of trust and respect. As you ensure trustworthiness of information and build effective communication (Chapter 5), you increase the level of trust and respect. As you remove the possibility of hidden agendas by aligning the purpose of all involved (Chapter 2), you increase the level of trust and respect. As you pay attention to systems and processes (Chapter 4), you increase the level of trust and respect.

## Knowing and Being Known

> For trust and respect to flourish you need to know and respond to whatever it takes for each participant in your venture to trust and respect.

Consider how you approach a business relationship with your colleagues. Does it make a difference to you whether you have worked with them before? What do you focus on in determining whether and how to trust and respect your colleagues?

If others in the venture are new to you:

- Do you want to know something about them in advance of working with them, or do you prefer to experience them personally?
- Do you prefer to relate with your colleagues based on their professional credentials or their personal backgrounds?
- Do you prefer to have a personal reference from someone you have worked with in the past, or make your own judgment based on your first hand experience with the person?
- Do you approach the venture trusting and respecting these new colleagues automatically, or reserving trust and respect for those who earn it?

If you have worked previously with the others involved in the venture:

- Do you automatically judge them based on your previous experience, or do you allow that they, like you, may have grown and changed since your last venture?
- Do you hold grudges concerning your colleagues' past mistakes, or forgive them and offer a fresh start?

What do you provide to others about yourself? Is it easy for others to get to know you? What do your colleagues pick up about you on their own? What does your personal and professional 'calling card' look like? That is, how do you present yourself based on the combination of ingredients identified in Figure 13? Whatever your answers to these questions, others may answer differently from you. This means that establishing and maintaining trust and respect requires some conscious effort on your part.

| Your personal and professional 'calling card' impacts trust and respect | |
|---|---|
| ◆ *Professional expertise and accomplishments* | Your achievements, personal proficiency and competence, breadth and depth of experience, ability to add value to specific situations |
| ◆ *Positional role and authority* | Your personal accountability, function, responsibility, title, command of resources and tools |
| ◆ *Personal character and reputation* | Your personal attributes, trustworthiness, interpersonal skills, follow through on commitments, ability to be counted on by others |

Fig. 13. Personal and professional calling card.

> You must manage your expectations about your colleagues, and help them to manage theirs about you.

You can start by ensuring that participants are acquainted with each other. Whether your venture is large or small, local or global, whatever you can do to help participants get familiar and comfortable with each other will serve to develop trust and respect among them.

Depending on whether you have all worked together before, and on how you and your colleagues develop trust and respect with others, a variety of tools can help you. These include:
- review of professional resumés
- facilitated discussions
- personality profiling and self-discovery tools such as Myers-Briggs Type Indicator® and Strengths Deployment Inventory®
- social events
- teambuilding sessions
- informal conversations
- having lunch together.

**Case study:   Partnering relationship begins with introductions** _____

To kick off one business partnering relationship, principals from four companies gathered for dinner. Some had worked together previously while others were newcomers to the group.

To expedite the process of getting acquainted and incorporating the new players as part of the team, individuals were given worksheets to complete about their colleagues. Then each participant introduced one colleague to the group based on answers to the questions. By doing this:

♦ Participants were formally introduced to the group from another's point of view.

♦ Everyone participated in the introductions.

♦ Participants got to 'experience' each other publicly, and on common ground.

A little choreography in this situation did a lot to get the venture started in a positive way.   _____

## Creating Interdependence

A three-legged stool requires all three legs to be viable as a stool. At the same time, each leg contributes its share of the effort. So it is with collaboration across organizational boundaries.

> To build trust and respect, you need to ensure that each party contributes real value to the venture and that this value is magnified because of the venture.

Assuming a healthy relationship among the parties, you will achieve true partnering when participants are interdependent. Consider the characteristics of your venture against those shown in the table in Figure 14.

What type of relationship best describes your situation? Can you say that the whole is greater than the sum of its parts – that all involved are better together than they would be separately?

As you look at the participants in your venture – both individuals and organizations, including yourself – to what degree are you all:

| Type of relationship | Productivity value Based on number of organizations involved (N) | Characteristics of the relationship |
|---|---|---|
| *Dependence –* Individual(s)/ organization(s) is/are dependent on other(s) to survive | 0 – N The whole is less than the sum of its parts | 'Boss' – 'subordinate' relationship with clear leader(s) and follower(s) |
| *Independence –* Individual(s)/ organization(s) work independently | N The whole equals the sum of its parts | Contractual/'letter of the law' relationship with cohabitation of entities under one label |
| *Interdependence –* Individual(s)/ organization(s) interact appropriately with and contribute to the whole enterprise | N+ The whole is greater than the sum of its parts | Synergistic relationship with 'generative spirit' |

Fig. 14.   The value of interdependence.

| *Interdependent* | *Dependent* |
|---|---|
| rooted | adrift |
| self-supporting | confused |
| governing | insecure |
| skilled | clumsy |
| holistic | fragmented |
| engaged | isolated |
| giving | stingy |
| peaceful | troubled |

Just as there are many ways to create a common purpose (Chapter 2) there are many correct ways to balance the level of autonomy and dependence in a collaborative business venture to create an interdependent relationship. What is appropriate for one collaborative venture may not work well at all in another. Let your own assessment provide you with guidance regarding how you might best spend your time to improve trust and respect in your venture. You will want to help move yourself and your colleagues toward interdependence.

**Case study:   Medical technicians and physicians work to improve trust and respect** _____

In one health care organization significant barriers existed among medical staff, administrators and technicians. Obvious boundaries and barriers had been created by the three independent organizational entities involved. The individuals had erected even greater barriers by their own words and deeds on a daily basis.

Members of each group reported that the others did not 'respect' or 'trust' them. Physicians highlighted that their authority and expertise were being questioned and undermined. Administrators expressed concerns that they had no authority or power to manage according to their stated responsibilities. Medical technicians reported being questioned as to their competency and behavior, and being micromanaged by both administrators and physicians.

The turning point in this collaborative venture came when representatives from all three organizations worked together to define success for the venture as a whole, and to establish some ground rules for their daily interactions. Through facilitated discussion, all had a voice in creating the desired future for the venture. Their work included:

◆ Reaffirmation of vision and mission for the venture.
◆ Validation of key roles, responsibilities, authorities for all involved.
◆ Development of a Code of Conduct for personal behavior.
◆ Revitalization of performance standards for all functions and personnel involved in the venture.

## Sharing Risk and Reward

One of the most effective ways to demonstrate trust and respect is to put your money where your mouth is. Mutual investment in success is clear evidence of trust and respect in collaborative ventures. Examples include:

◆ stock options
◆ revenue sharing
◆ profit sharing

- team bonuses
- incentive compensation.

To recognize or reward individual achievement or heroics undermines collaboration. You need to reward what you want. If you want individuals and organizations to behave as a team, sharing information, supporting each other, pitching in when needed to get the job done, you do not want to set apart the contributions of one or some individuals or organizations. You must reinforce the notion that everyone's contribution is important for success.

> You want to create an environment where for one to succeed all must succeed.

To build teamwork and collaboration across organizational boundaries, align rewards and recognition with your intent. Specifically:

- Quantify performance expectations, including expectations for your venture regarding teamwork and collaboration. You and your colleagues must define or describe the behavior you want. Otherwise, whether or not people perform according to your desire is largely a matter of chance.
- Drive ongoing alignment of priorities, standards and performance expectations among participants. Put another way, make sure that your ongoing dialogue with colleagues includes conversation about how well the group is performing with respect to expectations.
- Provide incentives to all participants to strive for excellence. Ensure that all forms of recognition and compensation are based in part on desired collaboration. Reward what you want. While monetary reward may not be the only motivator for collaborative behavior, it certainly presents an obstacle to collaboration if it is paid out for other reasons.

Once you agree to align rewards and recognition with your desired level of collaboration, all involved need to have confidence that everyone else can and will perform. If not, trust and respect erodes quickly and most individuals and organizations will not want to 'carry' another for too long. To guard against this, do whatever it takes to ensure top-notch performance from all involved in your venture. As described in Chapter 4, you must follow through to monitor and manage performance, celebrate success, and deal with problems and conflicts. Trust, respect, and collaboration will fall apart quickly if performance problems are not dealt with effectively and efficiently.

**Case study:   Collaboration is hurt by presidential award** _____

In a changing market environment, one company changed its organization structure from three independent business units to one functionally based organization – operations, engineering, sales and marketing, customer service, human resources, and finance. Trust and teamwork among individuals remained fragile as all parties worked to find their places and a new equilibrium in the new organization.

The message from executive management was that the company should present one face to the customers, and that it should become an integrated, collaborative enterprise.

These words seemed shallow when two individuals were singled out for presidential awards. These awards were given based on their '*individual heroics in dealing with a specific customer situation*'. This action sent a strong message to everyone that the company valued individual efforts more than teamwork.

Executive management realized after the fact that to build the desired collaborative enterprise, recognition and reward must be aligned with the objective. _____

## Using Personality to Advantage

Both individuals and organizations have personalities – qualities, characteristics, attributes, strengths and weaknesses that are visible to those around us. These individual and organizational personalities show up in cross-organizational collaborative ventures. When personalities among the parties are found to be compatible or similar, not much time is spent on the subject. However, when disagreements or discomfort surface among individuals or organizations, personality differences are often blamed for many of the difficulties.

No doubt you have been described or have described others in a variety of ways – for example:

- analytical
- intuitive
- driver
- amiable
- decisive
- outgoing
- introvert
- charismatic
- managerial

- flexible
- approachable
- stubborn
- quiet
- pragmatic
- realistic
- structured
- friendly
- results-oriented.

These various qualities, characteristics and attributes, commonly described as personality traits are not good or bad in their own rights. What makes them good or bad, and effective or ineffective, is how all these traits of a given individual or organization behave both:

- as a complete package in the specific business situation
- in relation to those of the other parties to the collaboration.

How all the personality traits interact with each other makes them effective or not. Whether and how you honor the different personalities of individuals and organizations and work well with them impacts collaboration across organizational boundaries.

Notice that the preceding paragraph does not say 'change' others' personalities, but rather 'honor' and 'work well with them'.

## Looking at personalities

Consider the following four personalities in relation to your own:

- John is described as a traditionalist, stabilizer, consolidator type who works from a sense of responsibility, duty and loyalty. He learns in a step-by-step way to prepare for current and future application of knowledge. He can be counted on to provide timely output, and he is good at adhering to policies, procedures and standards.
- Sandy is a troubleshooter, negotiator, fire-fighter type who is action oriented. She is quick and clever. She learns through active involvement, on a just-in-time basis. She is excellent at handling out-of-the-ordinary and unexpected situations.
- Tom is more of a catalyst and spokesperson. He works by

energizing himself and others around values and inspirations. He learns for self-awareness through personalized and imaginative ways. He regularly provides special vision of possibilities.

♦ Darlene is a visionary type, a builder of sorts who works on ideas and concepts with ingenuity and logic. She learns by an impersonal and analytical process for personal mastery. She is the one to go to if you are looking for strategy or analysis.

Notice both the similarities and differences among these four personalities. For example, with respect to the personality preferences described by the Myers-Briggs Type Indicator®:

♦ John and Tom desire affiliation with others based on norms, standards or values.

♦ John and Sandy focus on data, concrete details and sensory experiences.

♦ Tom and Sandy share interests in understanding motives, theirs and those of others.

♦ Sandy and Darlene are the pragmatists who like to focus on goals.

♦ John and Darlene share an interest in structure.

♦ Darlene and Tom can envision possibilities based on ideas, abstractions, patterns and symbols.

Look at these four again. Does one of the four seem more familiar or comfortable to you? Which one? And why? Similarly, do any of the four examples seem strange or uncomfortable to you? Again, which one(s), and why?

It is possible and probable that the characteristics describing Tom, Darlene, John, and Sandy above can be used to describe you and your colleagues too. That may be why some seem more familiar and comfortable to you while others seem strange or uncomfortable. You have been here before . . .

## Characteristics of organizations

Now consider that the same characteristics can exist in organizations. For example:

♦ Company A is described as structured, bureaucratic, organized, a 'well oiled machine'.

♦ Function B is referred to as flexible, spontaneous,

entrepreneurial, able to do 'whatever it takes to get the job done'.

♦ Organization C is known to be a catalyst that helps others see possibilities, a group with 'high ideals'.

♦ Department D is described as logical, strategic and visionary, a group of 'rational thinkers'.

Sound familiar? Perhaps you have type-cast in your mind, or in conversation, a company, function, department or professional organization based on similar characteristics. If so, you probably have found that those with certain characteristics are naturally easier for you to work with than others.

## Learning to relate to different types

Admit it. There are some individuals and organizations with whom you find it easier to work. Perhaps they are more like you at core, or perhaps you have learned through years of experience how to be effective when faced with certain personalities.

You cannot just rest on your laurels. To build trust and respect among those involved in your collaborative venture, you need to learn how to relate to your colleagues where they are. Whether they are like Tom, Darlene, Sandy or John, or like Company A, Function B, Organization C or Department D, it is your job to:

♦ Speak so that your colleagues can hear you – make it easy for them to listen.

♦ Write with language your colleagues understand – don't make them have to translate.

♦ Listen to understand when your colleagues talk to you – ask for clarification when needed, and test both your assumptions and your understanding.

♦ Learn their language so that you can read what your colleagues write – don't guess.

♦ Seek to understand where your colleagues are coming from before you try to be understood by them – remember that in context all behavior makes sense.

♦ Expect that your colleagues have different perspectives from you – don't count on them to agree with you or to see things the same way that you do.

♦ Recognize that your colleagues have something special to

contribute to your collaborative venture – look for the unique positive value each of your colleagues contributes, and if necessary, help them to contribute their best.

♦ Appreciate and value the contributions of your colleagues – don't wait for them to love yours.

If needed:

♦ Use personality profiling tools to better understand both yourself and your colleagues.

♦ Increase your personal knowledge about human dynamics – read books or attend classes.

♦ Participate in teambuilding sessions with your colleagues.

♦ Ask your colleagues how your work and relationship can be made better.

Learn to genuinely value and appreciate your colleagues, individually and collectively. Practice respecting them.

Becoming a student of human behavior and interpersonal dynamics will help you to learn how to really connect with your colleagues in order to build trust and respect – both theirs and yours.

**Case study:   Executive appreciates different viewpoints** _____

One executive in a Silicon Valley company described his experience with building successful collaboration across organizational boundaries as follows:

'I have had to really evolve from being directive into using and appreciating other leadership styles and appreciating other ways of looking at things. Ten or fifteen years ago I had to have all the answers and be able to do everything myself. I didn't trust teams to do things; I just figured out what needed to be done and how it should be done and directed everyone to do it. Partnering has really helped me evolve into appreciating other points of view, and trusting the team to figure out what to do and how to do it.' _____

## Maintaining Your Personal Commitment to Trust and Respect

To build and maintain trust and respect, you must establish a connection between you and your colleagues – as much of a connection that is comfortable for all involved, or just enough to dislodge fear, uncertainty and doubt.

At some level, regardless of real or perceived barriers of any kind, you and your colleagues are looking for the same things from your participation in a collaborative business venture:

◆ Significance of contribution – in terms of the role you play, the tasks you accomplish, and/or the legacy you leave as a result of your participation in the venture.

◆ Acceptance and appreciation by others – in terms of the rewards and recognition, support and encouragement, and socialization.

Your ability to help others obtain significance and acceptance will both result in significance and acceptance for you, and build trust and respect among all involved.

> If you help your colleagues get what they want as you get what you want, you will achieve successful collaboration across organizational boundaries.

To create and maintain trust and respect, be conscious of what your colleagues are trying to achieve and relate to them where they are. Keep your colleagues' hopes, wants, needs and expectations on your 'radar screen' – in every interaction. Then make it your business to genuinely connect with them. To do so:

◆ your words must connect with their definitions
◆ your interpersonal behavior must be acceptable to your colleagues
◆ your actions must be in concert with theirs.

> To create more trust and respect in your collaborative venture, give others more trust and respect.

This can be difficult if you are used to working independently or to being in positions of power and control. You might be used to having things your own way, without regard for others. If so, you will change; you now have an additional responsibility to care about your colleagues.

**Case study:   General manager learns to trust the team** _____

Halfway through a major fast-track construction project the general contractor executive was promoted to become the Group Chief Executive of his firm. This meant that a new Managing Director had to be appointed for the project.

The man who was chosen was accomplished, credentialed and appropriate for the role. He was skilled at directing others and entered the project with his own expectations about

- what should be done
- how things should be done
- who should be doing things.

At the same time he had not participated in shaping the initial business partnering relationship involving the general contractor and subcontractors, architects and consultants, and owner's representatives. As a result, when things were not proceeding in a way that was familiar and comfortable to him, his natural reaction was to try to change them to fit his model.

The team pushed back. They asked to be given a chance – to be trusted to do the right job in the right way.

The Managing Director found that when he modified his own behavior to trust the team more, to serve as a coach and mentor rather than to direct individual activities, participants in this venture could be trusted. The result was a successful project and important lessons learned. _____

## Key Tools and Techniques

To build trust and respect in your collaborative venture:

- ✔ Create one focus for participants by ensuring a common purpose, complete context and clear measures of success.
- ✔ Incorporate explicit mechanisms to build familiarity and comfort of relationship among participants – for example facilitated dialogue, personality profiling, social events.
- ✔ Agree on a code of conduct for those involved in your venture.
- ✔ Do your part to ensure competence among all participants in the venture.
- ✔ Ensure that all information you provide to others is trustworthy.
- ✔ Share risk and reward for your venture, and align reward and recognition to promote teamwork and collaboration among participants.
- ✔ Become a student of personality, human behavior and interpersonal dynamics so that you can relate appropriately to your colleagues.

CHAPTER 7

# Adaptability to Learn and Change

G iven the dynamics of most industries today, the need to deal with change is increasingly important. Some say that the only constant is change, and that the pace of change is increasing. Change is ever present and pervasive. It permeates your collaborative venture.

At a global level you are faced with such forces as:

- ◆ technological advances
- ◆ economic shifts
- ◆ new and different competitors
- ◆ changes in customers and markets
- ◆ social and political changes.

At the local level you must consider:

- ◆ the effects of personnel changes
- ◆ shifts in business priorities
- ◆ your customers' changing needs
- ◆ changes within the organizations participating in your venture.

These factors create both hazards and opportunities for your collaborative venture.

> To survive and even thrive in the face of all these changes you and your colleagues must be able to learn and change.

You must maintain high degrees of flexibility and agility in your systems, processes, people and structure.

## Incorporating a Change Mentality

Dealing with change is an area where both individuals and organizations behave differently:

- ◆ Some navigate through changes quickly and effortlessly. They seem to easily grasp a new vision or guidance to move in another direction and do so. They are happy to be first in moving forward.

◆ Some move smoothly, once the path is known. They need very little direction and rationale in order to move forward.

◆ Some move more carefully, or labor heavily along the way. They need very clear direction and rationale. They need to have confidence that all will be well, and that they are not alone.

◆ Some drag their feet or opt out at any step of the way. They may have a hard time letting go of the past or understanding why change is necessary. They may believe things are fine just as they are. They may appear reluctant, skeptical or afraid.

To complicate matters, both individuals and organizations behave differently depending on the nature of the change. They might move easily and quickly in one circumstance, but drag their feet in another. The more individuals or organizations perceive they have something to lose, the more likely they will be reluctant to change.

Even so, one of the factors that distinguishes successful collaborative ventures from others is the ability to foresee changes and navigate together a course of action. To do this, you and your colleagues must be in a state of readiness for change – both individually and organizationally. You and your colleagues must be:

◆ competent – able to perform the work at hand
◆ committed – willing to move forward
◆ courageous – motivated enough to take action.

If individual or organizational competence is threatened in any way, commitment and courage decline. This means that you must invest in education and training on an ongoing basis to ensure that you and your colleagues remain current and competent as circumstances change. Similarly, if motivation is not sufficient, no amount of competence will force the change. This means that you must ensure that you and your colleagues are appropriately motivated to move forward. Thirdly, if commitment is not present, change will not happen. This is why checking for alignment on a regular basis is so important. You and your colleagues will change only when you are committed to doing so.

Knowing these facts, you need to consider how you and your colleagues will deal with change together. Will you choose to:

- influence and shape your future by being proactive
- react appropriately when faced with changes
- remain at the mercy of whatever is going on around you?

You and your colleagues need to spend some time looking forward, thinking about the future and the changes you are likely to face. Defining your aptitude and attitude toward change up front helps collaboration on many fronts. By knowing something about how you will all deal with change, you can choose to:

- Strengthen the group's ability to perform.
- Clarify the process for how you will all go about being proactive or reactive – just enough for all involved in your venture to have what they need to be able to move forward.
- Build trust and respect by understanding and valuing both similarities and differences among individuals and organizations.

Whatever you choose, it is a choice. Whether and how well your collaboration works depends on your having a common understanding of how you will work together, even in the face of change.

**Case study:   Leader sets tone for collaborative venture** _____

At the beginning of one collaborative venture involving three companies, one of the key leaders set the tone for the group. He described the context for the venture, the business circumstances his company was facing, and his desires for the venture:

'The pace of change is accelerating. This group needs to be flexible to deal rapidly with changing dynamics. We are faced with competitive pressures, and our customers' needs continue to change. My measure of success for this venture includes how well and how rapidly we all will be able to respond to the changes we will face.

Communication will be critical for us. And we must check for alignment regularly. We will not be able to assume that just because we did something yesterday that it will apply tomorrow.' _____

## Using an Institutional Memory

To ensure that all involved in your venture learn and change, and to build collaboration across organizational boundaries, a steady flow of information must exist. You must get data, information, knowledge and wisdom out of individuals' heads or personal file drawers and into a form that all involved in your venture can use. You need some sort of institutional memory or central repository for information.

As described in Chapter 5, a central repository of information enhances communication by providing a 'home base' which you and your colleagues can visit to retrieve what you need. Additionally, as shown in Figure 15, a central repository supports individual and group learning and change through:

♦ Reference and research – common memory for historical background, context, policies, procedures and guidelines.

♦ Analysis and decision making – shared tools for real time modeling and report writing to clarify thoughts and ideas, codify documentation and justification, provide guidance and direction.

♦ Performance management – timely tracking and reporting of actual versus planned.

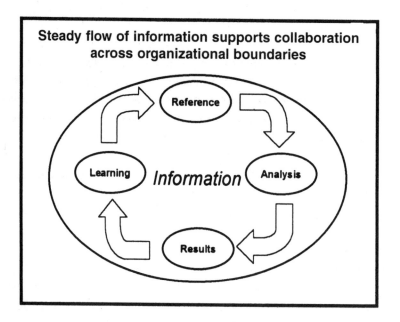

Fig. 15.   Information flow.

◆ Learning intervention – focal point for reflection on recent experiences.

To build an institutional memory for your collaborative venture, consider both:

◆ Collection of information – what kinds of information you and your colleagues have and need – text, numeric data, pictures, videos, drawings, models, etc; in what form(s) the information exists; how, where, when and by whom the information gets collected; where and how the information should be stored for use.

◆ Distribution of information – what you and your colleagues want to be able to do with the information; who needs access to the information, and how frequently; what security measures you need to protect your information.

There is a job to be done in actually organizing and managing this memory for the good of the venture.

Depending on the complexity of your venture you will need different tools and techniques to help you create and maintain your institutional memory. As shown in Figure 16, you need to add elements to your institutional memory as the size and complexity of your venture grows. Examine the continuum shown in the figure to match your situation with an appropriate selection of tools and techniques.

**Case study:  Knowledge management system captures lessons learned __**

Executives involved in one global collaborative venture determined that they needed an Internet-based knowledge management system to facilitate collaboration across six major locations around the world. Key to their system was the ability to capture lessons learned from project-related and operational experiences. They wanted everyone involved to benefit from lessons learned in order to both locally and globally:

◆ improve quality
◆ enhance service
◆ reduce costs.

They also wanted to ensure that all involved were working with common policies, procedures and guidelines to avoid unnecessary rework, and to make timely,

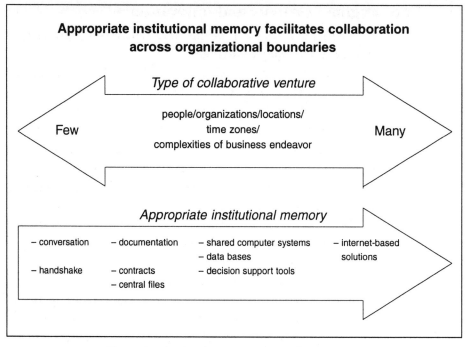

Fig. 16. Institutional memory tools and techniques.

informed decisions in the context of the bigger picture.

This team engaged an Internet specialist to design a system to:

◆ Capture, store and integrate a combination of text documents, financial spreadsheets, graphics and presentation materials, pictures, email messages, drawings and video, all indexed and accessible worldwide by those authorized to use the information.

◆ Retrieve any or all elements of the information contained in this knowledge management system according to their key work processes:

  – develop strategy – plan for future activities
  – deliver results – perform tasks, monitor and manage performance
  – manage resources – incorporate asset management, capital investment, risk management, budgeting and financial reporting
  – manage relationships – keep in contact with others
  – manage knowledge – ensure a learning organization.

As specific lessons are learned by team members, a dialogue and review process determines whether and how to include these as part of the institutional memory. By working with common information, this group is able to collaborate around the world. _____

# Encouraging Creativity and Innovation

Creativity and innovation captures hearts and minds, and builds individual and group commitment.

> If you do not foster creativity and innovation, the waves of change are likely to pass you by or obliterate your venture.

To determine whether and how you and your colleagues are encouraging creativity and innovation, take a look at the nature of your meetings, conference calls and correspondence. Look at how much time and energy is spent on:

- ◆ Past – reporting, reviewing, discussing, re-hashing or justifying past events either for their own sake or as a matter of reference for current or future activities.
- ◆ Present – commissioning action items or assignments, resolving problems or conflicts, or directing current activities.
- ◆ Future – brainstorming, planning, breakthrough thinking, and considering possibilities and alternatives for moving forward.

If the majority of your time and energy is spent reliving historical events, or dealing with problems or conflicts, you might want to infuse some creativity into your venture.

Also look at the decision-making and approval process for your venture. What does it take to get to 'yes'? And when and why do you or your colleagues say 'no'? How open are you and your colleagues to new ideas? Depending on your answers to these questions you and your colleagues may be limiting possibilities for real collaboration.

## *Taking some simple steps*

To encourage creativity and innovation, begin with the following simple steps:

- ◆ Question the status quo. Just because you and your colleagues have always done something in a particular way does not mean that it is the best approach for moving forward. As you question status quo, be sure to honor the value of the past and those who have contributed to make your group's efforts successful to date, and take time to build consensus regarding how best to move forward.

- Spend more time before taking action to look with your colleagues at possible scenarios with respect to both what needs to be accomplished and how best to do so. Consciously generate more alternatives than you need; rule them out only after you and your colleagues have explicitly articulated pros and cons of each.
- Actively explore as a group on a regular basis what you and your colleagues can stop, start or change. This is often difficult, even for successful individuals. The familiar is comfortable, and conventional wisdom says, 'if it ain't broke, leave it alone'. Unconventional wisdom says otherwise, however. You and your colleagues need to examine and change things while you can.

### Creating a nurturing environment

To infuse more creativity you must maintain a nurturing environment. If you or your colleagues find that when you offer an idea you get 'shot down' with verbal insults, laughter, criticism, or by being ignored, you are not likely to contribute anything of value. Conversely, if you and your colleagues find that you are encouraged to contribute new ideas, you will.

Part of this nurturing environment is physical. Some describe being creative as 'thinking outside the box'. In a physical sense you also need room to move outside the box. Make sure that:

- Meetings or conference calls allow ample time, with adequate space on the agenda for generative work.
- The physical space for your meetings and work sessions supports creativity and innovation. Meeting rooms that are sterile, small, poorly lit, noisy and with poor air circulation are not conducive to generative work. Meeting rooms should:
  - be large enough so that participants can be seated or move around easily
  - allow for any refreshments to be served in the room
  - incorporate lots of facilities for visual aids – slides, transparencies, models, flips charts, white boards, etc
  - be set round, square, or u-shaped, so that all participants can see each other easily. If the group is too large, use multiple round or square tables so that subgroups can benefit from this.

◆ Notes are captured in writing so that, when memories fade, there is a record of agreements, ideas and action plans.

Remember, too, that you must create an appropriate balance between freedom and control. Processes that are too centralized and bureaucratic stifle initiative and innovation. A better approach to build collaboration is to distribute as much authority as possible to collaborative work groups. Before turning them loose, clarify expectations and boundaries, and provide guidance regarding tools and techniques such as:

◆ brainstorming
◆ facilitation
◆ creative thinking
◆ constructive criticism.

**Case study: Everyone's ideas led to a better boat** _____

With architectural drawings in hand, Bill and Diane signed a contract to have a sailboat built. The builder came highly recommended. In advance of signing the contract, the couple talked to other boat owners and sailed on one of this builder's custom-designed boats. They spent time with the builder and his team to understand philosophy and core values, building process, ability of the team to perform, how communication would be accomplished, and what to expect from the experience. They proceeded based on trust and confidence in:

◆ What they were trying to do – a common purpose and vision for success.
◆ Who the people were – mutual trust and respect, and confidence in the team's ability to do the job.
◆ How the group would work together – defined processes and a plan for communication throughout the project.

Little did Bill and Diane know at the onset what a joy-filled collaborative adventure they had begun. Throughout the construction process, everyone had good ideas to make the sailboat identified by drawings, even better. Cabinetmakers, steelworkers, electronics and refrigeration experts, interior specialists, and owner, all had suggestions worthy of consideration.

The spirit of this collaboration was that everyone's voice was heard. For example, during a discussion about appropriate size and shape for a table the furniture maker volunteered to make up a sample real time. His work contributed directly to both a creative solution and a speedy decision. Similarly, others contributed suggestions and recommendations about sizes and shapes of doors and hatches, selection of deck hardware, type and placement of non-skid material. All are examples of the team members' creativity and of their confidence in the partnering process to know their ideas would be respected.

Even when Bill and Diane were not onsite they were able to participate in conference calls and email dialogues, and view digital pictures forwarded to them over the Internet.

Big and small, costly and inexpensive, aesthetic and functional, ideas flowed over the course of the 18-month construction period. Discussion and decision-making were timely, allowing the project to stay on schedule and within budget. And the resulting product is what the entire group describes as 'outstanding'.

What made this work is that all involved were competent, committed, and courageous enough to contribute ideas and participate in discussion regarding how to proceed. All were encouraged from the beginning to think, and to make this a great boat. The entire group benefited from:

◆ Common purpose in that all wanted to create a great boat.
◆ Performance day-by-day where everyone involved took pride in their work.
◆ Process which encouraged everyone's creativity and innovation.
◆ Effective communication using a combination of tools and techniques.
◆ Mutual trust and respect among all parties involved._____

## Committing to Continuous Improvement

'Good, better, best, and may you never rest, until your good is better, and your better, best'. So goes the old saying, but what about you and your colleagues? Are you resting or are you reaching to become better, or even best?

World-class? Best in class? Better than last year? What is your objective and how do you know that you are making progress?

All enterprises are growing or dying. They must be doing one or the other, and they cannot be doing both at the same time. By standing still, you and your colleagues issue a death sentence for your collaborative venture. *You need improvement goals.*

First, systematize so that you pay attention to what you are doing. Know what is going on. You cannot improve what you do not know. As described in Chapter 4, there are many ways to define and track performance.

Next, consider what your goals should be regarding:

◆ higher standards
◆ faster turnaround

- reduced costs
- improved quality
- enhanced service
- new capabilities.

Thirdly, clarify the rationale for these improvement goals – why they are important – and understand whether and why these goals are:

- Internally motivated, focused on improvement over your own existing measurements.
- Externally motivated, focused on meeting or beating competitive, industry benchmarks.

Finally, commit to getting better – both with respect to what you are doing and how you are doing it. Make sure that you and your colleagues establish appropriate improvement plans, and that you follow through on your commitments.

**Case study: Even an award-winning team would improve next time** ____
At the conclusion of one 12-month collaborative venture, the team was given a national award for project partnering. Even so, the core team of nine executives representing five companies identified the following improvements to be made for future ventures:

- Start the partnering process earlier by assembling the core team earlier, and using partnering concepts to recruit members to the team.
- Enhance the core team to include a couple of additional key participants.
- Set and manage expectations better for all involved by developing full understanding and commitment to partnering.
- Use technology better for correspondence and communication, by making sure that all understand how to use it.
- Achieve continuous improvement by performing analysis, setting clear improvement goals and using benchmarking techniques to provide guideposts.
- Clarify the organizational structure earlier._____

## Incorporating Learning

In successful business partnering relationships across organizational boundaries, people and organizations grow and develop. They learn from their experiences and from each other.

And they apply their learning to new activities. This benefits the venture itself as well as all the individuals and organizations involved.

Shared experiences help to build bonds among participants, and provide common background and context from which to move forward. Actively incorporating learning ensures a foundation for managing change.

How do you know that participants in your venture are learning? What evidence do you have? And, rather than merely academic exercise, how do you know that they are incorporating what they learn for the good of your venture?

> To incorporate learning explicitly in your collaborative venture, you must design the venture for it.

As you craft the governance rules for your business partnering relationship, you should include some guidance about how you will manage your learning together. To do so, you must agree on how you want to treat learning. What you decide may very well influence:

- Underlying values, vision and purpose for your venture.
- Key processes, systems, tools and techniques that you employ for your work together on a daily basis.
- How you measure success and manage expectations for your venture.
- Selection and retention of individuals and organizations to be involved in the collaborative effort.
- Whether and how you incorporate specific learning interventions as part of your work together.
- How you collect, store and disseminate information among individuals and organizations.
- Types of reward and recognition for your venture.
- How you treat mistakes along the way.

If your collaborative venture is for a short-term, discrete project your decisions may be different from if you are involved in a sustaining, long-term business relationship. Even so, by helping participants to learn and grow together you will build collaboration across organizational boundaries.

**Case study:   Turnaround is based on lessons learned**_____

Before calling it quits on a business partnering relationship after a bad experience working together, principals from three companies decided to give their relationship one more try. They:

◆ Articulated all their lessons learned from their previous experience.
◆ Went back to the basics regarding what is partnering
  - alignment of purpose
  - ability to perform
  - attention to process
  - acuity of communication
  - attitude of trust and respect
  - adaptability to learn and change.
◆ Decided to enhance some key processes and break down some barriers that had existed among participants.
◆ Made promises to each other regarding what would be different this time.
◆ Began again.

They were committed to turn around this business relationship, and they did. Their lessons learned turned into real learning – for mutual benefit. _____

# Key Tools and Techniques

To ensure that your collaborative venture maintains flexibility and agility to deal with the forces of change:

✔ Create a common institutional memory so that all participants have access to key information.

✔ Encourage creativity and innovation by dedication of time, energy, environment and attitude.

✔ Commit to continuous improvement throughout the life of your venture. Set specific goals and monitor progress toward improvements in both:
  - what you are doing
  - how you are going about it.

✔ Actively incorporate learning into new activities. Manage knowledge explicitly so that it can be applied easily to changing circumstances.

✔ Develop a change mentality for your venture so that all involved expect to learn and change.

Part 2

# Making Successful Collaboration Happen

CHAPTER 8

# Getting Started

I f you are serious about *Partnering in Action*, you will not you leave collaboration to chance. You will influence the outcome by paying attention to the six key elements. You will ensure that in your venture there is:

- alignment of purpose
- ability to perform
- attention to process
- acuity of communication
- attitude of trust and respect
- adaptability to learn and change.

Put simply, to develop and maintain successful collaboration across organizational boundaries, you need to be sure that you and your colleagues know and support:

- what you are trying to achieve
- who is doing what to whom
- how you are going to get the job done successfully.

It does not matter whether you are starting a new venture from scratch, merging otherwise successful ventures into one, or energizing a venture that is faltering. As depicted in Figure 17, in order to create and maintain successful collaboration across organizational boundaries you must create an alignment among people, purpose and practice.

Notice that in Figure 17 any reference to organizational boundaries is omitted. This is important. To develop and maintain collaboration across organizational boundaries you must minimize the importance of such boundaries and focus instead on *what you are trying to create together*. Concentrate on:

- The people involved – who they are with respect to your venture, and all of what they represent including their home organizations.

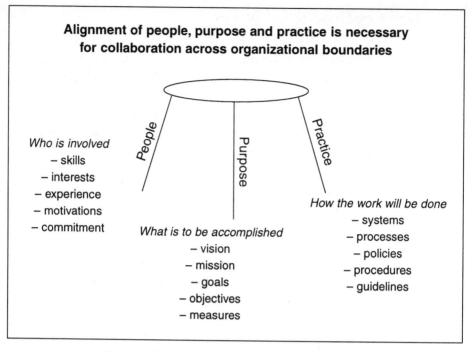

**Alignment of people, purpose and practice is necessary for collaboration across organizational boundaries**

*People*

*Purpose*

*Practice*

*Who is involved*
  – skills
  – interests
  – experience
  – motivations
  – commitment

*What is to be accomplished*
  – vision
  – mission
  – goals
  – objectives
  – measures

*How the work will be done*
  – systems
  – processes
  – policies
  – procedures
  – guidelines

Fig. 17.   Alignment of people, purpose and practice.

♦ The purpose to be achieved from your combined efforts, rather than those of any one of the organizations separately.

♦ The practice for your venture, building on best practices from each of the contributing organizations, but not necessarily relying unilaterally on those of any one organization.

The more closely aligned you and your colleagues are around people, purpose and practice, the easier it should be to establish and maintain collaboration across organizational boundaries. The more these are different, the more work you will need to do up front in order to define a relationship that is workable for all involved.

To assist you in creating alignment among the organizations involved in your venture, a cultural alignment worksheet is included as Appendix D of this book. You can use this worksheet to help you:

♦ Examine similarities and differences of prospective partners.

♦ Develop with your colleagues a plan for your venture to address specific items concerning purpose, people and practice.

♦ Clarify and understand root causes of difficulties in a faltering collaborative venture.

# Defining Criteria for Success

In Chapter 2 you read about the importance of a common purpose, the need to neutralize biases and hidden agendas of individual constituencies, and the significance of well-defined objectives. Here is where you put those ideas into practice.

To ensure successful collaboration across organizational boundaries you must ensure that all are clear on what success will look like for your venture:

- How you all will know that you have accomplished your mission.
- What evidence will demonstrate that you have made progress along the way.

However big or small, measurable or fuzzy, long-term or immediate, the more you can do to instill one picture in the minds and hearts of all involved in your venture, the more likely you will be to experience true collaboration. This picture must be:

- finite
- sharp
- vibrant
- crisp
- concise
- compelling.

All involved need to have the same picture in mind – the same target. You and your colleagues need to know how your respective activities contribute to reaching this target, and when and whether you are making progress toward it. These pieces of the picture comprise success criteria. They should be:

- well-defined
- measurable
- related to individual activities.

Note that these success criteria should include measures of *what* you and your colleagues are doing as well as *how* you are doing so together; something about the tasks involved plus the relationships to be managed. Consider the sample measures in Figure 18.

Some would call the 'how' the 'soft skills'. For most of us these

| Measures of Success | |
|---|---|
| *Sample task measures* | *Sample relationship measures* |
| ◆ Completed on time<br>◆ Within budget<br>◆ According to specifications<br>◆ Quality standards met<br>◆ Results orientation<br>◆ No excuses | ◆ Level of teamwork<br>◆ Common courtesy<br>◆ Effective communication<br>◆ Follow through on commitments<br>◆ Service mentality<br>◆ 'Can do' attitude<br>◆ Good judgment |

Fig. 18. Sample measures of success.

are the hard ones, particularly in cross-organizational collaborative ventures.

Finding the appropriate balance in measures of success for those involved in your venture between 'soft' and 'hard', between 'what' and 'how', between tasks and relationships is critical for success.

### Case study:   Principals involved in collaborative venture set criteria for success

For one venture involving more than ten companies, 12 months, and $60 million, the core team identified the following seven success criteria and accompanying measurements.

| *Success factor* | *As measured by . . .* |
|---|---|
| ◆ Business objectives, schedules and budget are met | ◆ Achieving scope, budget and schedule as approved initially |
| ◆ Design objectives are met | ◆ Semi-monthly core team dialogue<br>◆ Peer acclaim<br>◆ Minimal rework |
| ◆ Cross-organizational team establishes and maintains an effective communication process for the life of the venture | ◆ Semi-monthly core team dialogue<br>◆ Speed and clarity of written communication among the group<br>◆ Level of timely follow-through on action items from all meetings |

- Venture is a financial success for all involved

- Venture creates a model for future success in terms of language
  example
  example

- Every team member has a sense of personal satisfaction

- This venture is fun

- Benchmarking and peer feedback
- Performance-based compensation for the entire team
- Invitations by others to explain our success (eg speeches, references, articles, etc)
- Peer recognition
- Our methods are copied in the future
- Semi-monthly core team dialogue
- Mutual willingness to write letters of recommendation for each other
- Comments and feedback from team members – survey and anecdotal
- Milestone events
- Recurring feedback from team members

Members of the core team for this venture relied heavily on semi-monthly meetings to help them ensure that the venture remained on track. At each of their meetings they dealt with both the 'what' of the venture and the 'how', both the 'hard' deliverables and the 'soft' ones. _____

## Initiating *Partnering in Action*

The best way to get you and your colleagues on the 'same page' is to get you in the same room. You need to take time together to:

- Discuss, explore and evolve definition and direction for your venture.
- Experience each other, get acquainted, and build mutual trust and respect.
- Define how you will measure success for your venture.
- Gain agreement on purpose, priorities, and principles.
- Clarify how you will work together on a daily basis.

Whether informal or formal, short or long, the time you spend together up front will pay dividends throughout the life of your venture.

You may need to fight the temptation to 'just get on with it'.

Please do. If you do not take the time to do this right at first, you will have to make time to do it later. This is where, as one executive put it, 'you have to go slow to go fast'. Harnessing the excellence of each individual and organization for your venture can be a lot like lassoing wild stallions. Each must be treated individually, and with care.

If you now are restarting a faltering venture, your job may be even more complicated. Instead of having a blank sheet of paper on which to craft the direction for your venture, you may first need to undo the previous experiences.

Based on the size of your venture, it may not be feasible to have everyone participate in the initial discussions. This is when your core team proves valuable. Just like representative government, the core team can be empowered to provide guidance and direction for the venture.

## Getting focused

Regardless if all can participate or if a core team represents the entire venture, and regardless of whether the venture is new or starting again, many have found that one or more dedicated work sessions help(s) to get everyone focused. Some call these **partnering workshops**; others call them **strategy planning work sessions**; still others simply call them offsite meetings. Whatever they are called, this event or series of events is important to set the stage for successful collaboration.

To be of most value, such a meeting or work session needs to be:

♦ Structured just enough for those involved (some need more, some need less).
♦ Facilitated by a professional who is familiar with both content and process, respected by the participants and yet outside of the group.
♦ Conducted in a setting that is supportive of the work session's objectives.

Your agenda should be three-fold:

♦ Clarify expectations for the venture.
♦ Establish high-level ground rules to define how your venture will operate.
♦ Obtain alignment and participants' commitments for moving forward.

The primary deliverable from each event should be a summary document that highlights agreements and action items.

The key is that each work session needs to be generative. You and your colleagues must all participate. Together, you must:

- Define words to determine the language for your venture.
- Agree on specific measures for success.
- Determine how you will work together moving forward.
- Demonstrate your personal and organizational commitments to the venture.
- Build confidence and support among all involved.

**Case study: Successful venture uses partnering workshop as kickoff event** _____

Following the merger of two companies, executives were faced with the need to integrate many employees, outside consultants and contractors from both companies into one fast-track project with a budget of $50 million. To do so, they convened a core team of 15 people in a one-day partnering workshop with the following agenda:

1 Ensure common objectives for this team, including success requirements for all individuals and organizations involved.
2 Establish key ground rules for partnering.
3 Obtain alignment and participants' personal commitments for moving forward.

During the course of their meeting participants identified the following objectives for their work together:

- This project is delivered on schedule, within budget and according to agreed specifications.
- The journey / process is comfortable for all involved.
- We exceed expectations by creating delight and comfort for our customer, this entire team, community and management.
- This project creates a competitive advantage for all involved.
- We provide good business value.

They created their own 'recipe' for collaboration:

- communication
- Helping each other
  - asking for it
  - providing it
  - accepting it

- accountability (team and individual)
- understanding each other / get to know personalities, skills, expectations, limitations.

They clarified individual and organizational roles and accountabilities, and identified key action items for moving forward together. They also agreed to meet on a regular basis to ensure that they stayed on track.

The result? A very successful project of which everyone was proud._____

## Implementing Proactive Systems and Structures

You and your colleagues will have some means and mechanisms by which work gets done (or does not get done) for your venture. The question is whether or not these means and mechanisms will be:

- explicit or implicit
- overt or covert
- proactive or reactive.

In Chapter 4 you read about some key processes that influence collaboration across organizational boundaries. At a minimum you want be able to:

- Offer a crisp definition for your venture by making milestones visible.
- Manage the collaborative relationship itself.
- Employ effective meeting management techniques.
- Monitor progress throughout the life of your venture.
- Solve problems and manage conflicts as they arise.

You can save yourself a lot of pain if you take the time and energy up front to define and develop whatever systems and structures you and your colleagues need to work well together. Examples include:

- tracking systems and reports
- common computer systems with appropriate communication links
- data bases and files
- standing meetings and conference calls
- management reporting structure.

It is not necessary to have every detail agreed; however, it is important to clarify whatever questions and concerns you or your colleagues have that may impact your ability to work well together.

### Case study: Worldwide collaborative venture balances global consistency with local requirements _____

To improve planning for a worldwide company, it was necessary to bring together the independent planning organizations from around the world to define and develop one integrated planning process. Their objective – global consistency and local flexibility.

The planning efforts for this company had grown as the company had grown – by merger and acquisition, in both geographic and functional areas, and with little direction from one corporate center. National boundaries, cultures and customs; functional organizations within the company; policies and procedures of standalone business units derived from independent predecessor companies – all played a role in shaping the existing planning process.

In order to improve the situation, planners from around the world convened in a series of work sessions. Together they:

◆ Articulated the global company requirements.
◆ Described and documented current practices.
◆ Identified idiosyncrasies of the local planning efforts.
◆ Clarified objectives for their work together.
◆ Developed a common vision for the future integrated system.
◆ Procured and developed the systems infrastructure necessary for moving forward.
◆ Created an implementation plan to both develop the required new system and transition from existing activities – including elements of global consistency, local flexibility, economies of scale, cost effectiveness, ease of use, ease of implementation and continuous improvement.
◆ Followed through to complete the implementation and monitor progress against objectives.

In order to collaborate across numerous boundaries including organizational, national, cultural and time zone, this group focused their efforts on both:

◆ What they needed to do to create one integrated planning process.
◆ How they accomplished their objectives by working together._____

## Incorporating a Recovery Mechanism

As described in Chapter 4 a recovery mechanism is critical for building collaboration across organizational boundaries. You should count on the fact that everything in your venture will not go as planned. For example:

- You or any of your colleagues will revert to non-collaborative behaviors.
- Business circumstances will change, rendering your plans and priorities null and void, and forcing tensions high among all involved in your venture.
- You or one of your colleagues will make a mistake.

> Whatever the issue, if you want collaboration to be strong in the face of adversity you need to manage everyone's expectations regarding what will happen when you or your colleagues blow it.

## Assessing Readiness to Proceed

Along the way, you need to be able to assess 'readiness' for your venture – readiness to move forward; readiness to change. If you move too quickly you will lose people along the way. Likewise, if you dawdle too long the venture may miss its window of opportunity.

To build collaboration across organizational boundaries you and your colleagues must be courageous, committed and competent to proceed:

- Competent – in function, form and fit, as described in Chapter 3.
- Committed – as evidenced by personal willingness to move forward.
- Courageous – as represented by personal motivation.

Often individuals will assess their own readiness as more than that of their colleagues. They will claim that their colleagues are not committed enough, or not competent to perform the work, or not motivated to do their parts.

Be on the lookout regarding whether you and your colleagues are ready to collaborate. When you sense that you or any of your colleagues are stuck, or to avoid being stuck, make sure that:

- Everyone involved is aligned around a common purpose for your venture.
- You and your colleagues are able to perform according to what needs to be done.
- Your chosen processes and systems serve the venture well.
- Communication flows openly, easily, and honestly among individuals and across organizational boundaries.
- There is a high degree of trust and respect among participants.
- Your venture is alive, and participants are growing and changing.

**Case study: Executives from two companies consider a collaborative relationship** _____

As executives from two companies prepared to meet to explore whether the companies might merge or create a formal alliance of some kind, they had already read the company brochures and annual reports. Now they had a seemingly miscellaneous potpourri of questions, yet very real with respect to building collaboration across organizational boundaries.

Following is an excerpt from their long list:

- How large is their sales force, what is their structure and how do they work?
- How does the company get its business?
- How is the sales team compensated?
- What does the company mean by the word 'replicate'?
- What would happen to our current clients?
- What would happen to our current suppliers?
- What would a merger look like to our clients and suppliers, and to theirs?
- What operational systems do they have in place, and how do they relate to ours?
- How do they envision operations to be after the merger?
- If we move forward together, how would we establish policies and procedures for the new company or would they expect us to use theirs?
- How are decisions made in their company?
- What is the distinction between partner and supplier?
- How have others faired in being acquired by the company?
- What's in this for them?
- How will we have to change what we are doing now?
- What is the real culture of the company?
- What kind of computer systems do they use?

Notice that the questions are all over the board – large and small; strategic and tactical; people related, systems related, philosophy related; from the customer's perspective and from a prospective employee's perspective. Also note that all questions are real until they are answered directly or until these executives feel comfortable that all is well.

People, purpose and practice must align for this collaborative relationship to be successful. _____

## Putting First Things First

There is no one way for making collaboration work across organizational boundaries. You must find common ground with your colleagues for your venture. You must focus on those aspects of collaboration that capture the interest and enthusiasm of the participants.

> If you are questioning where to begin to secure a successful business partnering relationship across organizational boundaries, begin with alignment of purpose.

Experience shows that when there is a common purpose, other factors fall in place more easily. Once purpose is clear and all participants are in agreement, focus on any of the other keys to collaboration as presented in this book.

Also, remember that to build collaboration people have to want to do so. Get people involved who have collaboration skills and interests. At the end of the day, if participants do not want to collaborate, nothing you can do will change that.

Above all, check for alignment – the common place among all involved. To build and enjoy the benefits of successful collaboration you need to get people working together. You do that from a common place.

If you or your colleagues have been doing other things or focusing on your own priorities, you may need to be convinced to change what you are doing and/or how you are doing things in order for this venture to succeed. It may be difficult for you or your colleagues to give up your current activities in favor of doing something else. Even so, it may be necessary for you to change your personal behavior if collaboration is to succeed.

**Case study: Three companies are merged into one under new management** _____

Following the merger of three companies into one, the new executive team had to move quickly to align the efforts of all involved. They had to examine:

- underlying corporate philosophy
- business value drivers
- business focus
- business strategy
- measures of profitability and success
- personnel policies
- compensation and benefits programs
- code of conduct
- facilities
- relationships with partners and suppliers
- decision-making process
- accountability
- information systems
- financial management and reporting systems and practices
- supply chain management practices
- sales process
- customer service practices
- communication tools and techniques
- rewards and recognition practices
- conflict and problem management practices.

Until the executives could provide clarity and focus for the new venture, employees of the former companies clung to their old familiar policies and procedures, and behaved in ways that served them well before the merger. In some cases these were harmonious; in others they were in direct conflict with each other. _____

# Key Tools and Techniques

To enjoy the benefits of successful collaboration in terms of high performance, cost effectiveness and personal satisfaction, you need to align people, purpose and practice early in the life of your venture. You must establish focus and clarity so that all involved know why, how and what you and your colleagues are trying to accomplish together. To do this:

✔ Agree on a common purpose, clear mission and measures of success.

✔ Ensure that all involved are competent with respect to function, form and fit needed for this venture, and that their roles and responsibilities are understood and accepted.

✔ Determine how you will govern the venture, including the 'vital few' key processes and systems to be used.

✔ Clarify up front what you all will do if and when things get off track.

✔ Check, and re-check, for alignment among participants regarding:
  - People – expectations of participants with respect to each other
  - Purpose – what this venture is trying to accomplish
  - Practice – how the group will go about its work.

CHAPTER 9

# Sustaining Your Collaboration

M uch of the time that an airplane is in flight it is off course. The autopilot or real pilot must correct the course at key intervals to ensure that the plane will arrive at its destination. The same is true with collaboration. In the busy-ness of the day you and your colleagues are likely to get off course. Mistakes will be made; participants will revert back to old behaviors, new participants will be added, etc. The question is 'So what, who cares? What will you do about it?'

To ensure that your collaborative venture stays that way you must:

◆ Follow through on your original good intentions.
◆ Recognize and encourage collaborative behavior.
◆ Make corrections and enhancements along the way.
◆ Be resolute if the going gets tough.

## Following Through on Good Intentions

Assuming that you have got off to a good start and that you and your colleagues have established some ground rules for your business partnering relationship, you have a basis for successful collaboration. That means that you now have a choice – you can follow through on your commitments and action plans, or not.

In order for collaboration to be successful across organizational boundaries you must do your part. You must make good on your commitments to behave according to what you and your colleagues have agreed. You also have a responsibility to help others follow through on their commitments regarding the desired collaborative behaviors.

When you or your colleagues do not follow the group's own rules, then the collective group must be able to rely on an established recovery mechanism to get individuals and organizations back on course.

**Case study:   Some do and some do not follow through on commitment to collaboration** _____

Two fast-track development projects in the high tech industry show an important contrast in follow-through. Both projects were approximately the same size in terms of overall budget and timeframe, and similar in scope. Both involved participants from three major companies along with many consultants, subcontractors and other organizations. Both projects convened strong core teams, comprising principals from the three major companies, and began with a facilitated partnering workshop to:

◆ Ensure common objectives for the project.
◆ Establish ground rules for how the project team would operate.
◆ Obtain commitments of both individuals and organizations.

Both projects were completed on time. Both achieved their task objectives. Yet core team members from one of the projects reported that the experience was not fun. They recounted sadly that they had not enjoyed working with each other, that they were disappointed in the process and that they would not like to do this again. Their venture had been fraught with mistakes and rework, which resulted in a budget overrun. They described a nagging 'punch list' of details still to be handled.

In contrast, core team members from the other project reported a happy experience. They discussed with pride and enthusiasm what they had learned on the project, how they had grown as individuals and as a team, and how they looked forward to working together again in the future. Their end result was delivered on time, within budget and with customer satisfaction.

Granted, a number of differences could have contributed to the difference in outcomes, including differences in:

◆ specific business context for each project
◆ stakeholders' expectations and pressures placed on the team
◆ the individuals who were involved
◆ cultures and expectations of the organizations involved.

At the same time, the core teams for these two projects described a notable difference in how they conducted their collaborative ventures:

◆ The team that sadly recounted the unhappy experience reported that all their meeting time, correspondence, conference calls and status reporting had been focused strictly on task. They had spent no time at all managing their relationships. They did not follow up on the commitments they had made early on about how they would work together. Rather, as individuals they grumbled and growled as colleagues' behavior fell short of their expectations, but they did nothing to change it. Essentially they left their collaboration to chance.

♦ In contrast, the team that joyfully described a satisfying experience reported that throughout the life of the venture the core team met face to face on a monthly basis not only to review performance on tasks, but also to:
  – check for continuing alignment among all parties with respect to values, goals, objective, and priorities
  – examine whether and how participants were behaving according to plan
  – create corrective action as needed.

Following through on good intentions made a real difference in outcome._____

## Going Back to Basics

Sustaining collaboration across organizational boundaries is a lot like caring for a garden. When you plant a garden, you must also plan for its upkeep if you want to realize the fruits of your investment. So it is with collaboration.

> For your business partnering relationships to thrive or even survive you must feed, water, weed and prune collaboration.

This means that you must:

♦ Establish a plan for how you and your colleagues will care for your collaboration on an ongoing basis – when, how, and who to feed, water, weed, prune, etc.

♦ Remain conscious of your chosen course of collaboration – the ground rules by which your venture will operate.

If you and your colleagues have established a solid foundation for your collaborative venture, then periodic 'gardening' should be straightforward. Your objectives should be to:

♦ Assess how well your venture is doing relative to the six key elements discussed in this book:
  – alignment of purpose
  – ability to perform
  – attention to process
  – acuity of communication
  – attitude of trust and respect

> – adaptability to learn and change.

- Ensure that you are following your own previously agreed rules for collaboration.
- Reinforce desired behaviors.
- Identify strengths and potential weaknesses for moving forward.
- Redirect where necessary to stay on course.
- Reconfirm participants' personal commitments to making your collaborative venture successful.

To help you, you can use a combination of:
- facilitated partnering work session
- survey feedback
- informal dialogue
- management by walking around
- core team discussion.

Involved in several cross-organizational collaborative business relationships, one executive and avid golfer summarizes the idea of going back to basics as follows: 'Here is where you must keep your eye on the ball, and the ball on the fairway.'

### Case study:   Partnering report card provides basis for discussion _____

To ensure that the venture stayed on track the core team for one collaborative venture invoked partnering report card on a periodic basis – monthly at first, migrating to quarterly over time.

Wanting to focus their attention on areas where the most good could be done, they chose to highlight which area 'needs attention now'.

Per the agreed schedule, each core team member filled out a partnering report card from his/her own perspective. The results were consolidated and submitted to the core team for discussion. A sample from one of their meetings is shown in Figure 19. Using their report card as a basis for discussion, the core team agreed that:

- The group seems to be working pretty well together.
- Focus for improvement should be placed on communication, with attention to really understanding._____

| Partnering Report Card | | |
|---|---|---|
| Key differentiators for partnering for this venture | Team grade for this period (one per box) (A, B, C, D, F) | Priority for improvement check one or more) |
| ◆ Communication among team members | B, B, B, B+, A–, C, A, B, B, A–, B, B, B | X, X, X, X, X, X, X, X |
| ◆ Helping each other | B, A, B, A–, B, A+, B, B, A, A, A, A, A | X, X, X |
| ◆ Accountability (team and individual) | A, A, A–, A, B, A, A, A, A+, B, A, A, A, A | X |
| ◆ Understanding each other – personality, skills, expectations, limitations | A, B, B, B+, B+, B, A, B, B, B, B+, A, A | X, X, X |

Fig. 19.   Sample partnering report card.

# Knowing What to Do When the Going Gets Tough

When the going gets tough, and it looks like individuals or organizations are just not going to behave in the agreed collaborative manner for whatever reason, you and your colleagues must decide what you will do about it. You can modify the ground rules for your venture to make the offending behavior acceptable, or you have three choices:

◆ Invoke the recovery mechanism, yet again.
◆ Escalate the situation, up to and including removing from the venture the offending individual(s) or organization(s).
◆ Remove yourself from this venture.

Remember, as described in Chapter 3, when others do not behave in the way you expect them to, it is because they:

◆ do not know what to do differently
◆ do not know how to do differently
◆ cannot do differently
◆ do not want to do differently.

If you are serious about your originally agreed collaboration, then accepting offending behavior is not an option for you. All of the wisdom about 'tough love' comes into play in this situation. You must take action to correct the situation. If you know that someone is not collaborating according to what you all have agreed, and you do nothing about it, then you are not collaborating either.

**Case study:   Business partnering relationship ends after many years** ____

For more than six years a business partnering relationship existed among three companies. The same key individuals worked together successfully on many projects. They had benefited themselves and their respective companies. Working together, the three companies repeatedly and predictably delivered results on time in a profitable manner due to their partnering skill:

◆ alignment of purpose
◆ ability to perform
◆ attention to process
◆ acuity of communication
◆ attitude of trust and respect
◆ adaptability to learn and change.

The principals involved from the three companies:

◆ Understood and appreciated common values, and infused each project with clear objectives and priorities.
◆ Respected each other as professionals and trusted each other as people.
◆ Built a reservoir of confidence in each others' ability to perform.
◆ Developed communication among the team so that with very little detail they could all execute their respective tasks in harmony.
◆ Defined key processes to allow them to work together effectively and efficiently across organizational boundaries.
◆ Captured lessons learned so that they could grow together.

However, when a key executive retired from one of the companies, all that changed. A new participant became involved in the venture on behalf of the firm. Additionally, the firm's culture began to change. The result was that three firms that used to work together well began to struggle to work together at all. Communication became strained, process was not honored, and trust and confidence were undermined and eroded by a combination of unspoken expectations and failure to follow through.

As they tried to rekindle this business partnering relationship, the principals from the three firms found too much of a mismatch now in purpose, people and practice. In short, with just one retirement a partnering relationship of long standing had to be dismantled. _____

## Celebrating Success

Acknowledging and applauding success along the way encourages participants to keep the collaborative efforts going. Yet this may not be so easy to do, there may be a lot working against you. For example:

♦ Most of you have probably got where you are because of your ability to solve problems, not notice success.

♦ Most of you just keep on going. You are used to getting things done, not reflecting on what you and your colleagues have accomplished. And if you do take time to look at what you are doing it is usually with the task in mind, not with respect to the quality of relationship you have with your colleagues.

♦ Bad news usually gets press. Most of you can be quick to point out when someone else does something wrong, but you may not be equally quick to notice when the same individual or organization does something really well.

At the same time:

♦ Those who want or need your attention probably know from past experience that they are likely to get it easily and quickly if they do something wrong, but can they count on getting recognition if they do something well?

♦ What incentive can be seen by those who are skeptical about the value of collaboration in the first place to do things other than by themselves?

♦ How will you protect and honor the contributions of those who are experts in their fields while encouraging collaboration?

♦ What allowances have you made within individual assignments, tools, resources, and/or time schedules to accommodate the time and energy required by individuals to work with others rather than by themselves?

The above lists point to the fact that in order to sustain collaboration across organizational boundaries you must provide reinforcement for you and your colleagues to do the right thing with respect to genuinely collaborating with others.

> You must develop the ability of everyone to notice and appreciate when you and your colleagues are doing things right.

Tools to help you celebrate success include:

◆ Peer review and feedback – may be done in writing or face to face, formally or informally, including specific items highlighting the desired collaborative behavior.

◆ Collaboration review – facilitated discussion regarding how things are going.

◆ After action briefings and lessons learned reviews – including discussion, description and wisdom for others regarding what went well with respect to collaboration as well as task.

◆ Partnering report card – a vehicle to provide an overall view of how things are going and a basis for discussion; effective in conjunction with facilitated discussion such as collaboration review or lessons learned review.

◆ Special awards and recognition – individualized for the situation, empowering all participants to provide positive feedback.

◆ Core team meetings – including a topic on the agenda for participants to articulate and recognize what aspects of collaboration are going well.

◆ Milestone events – whatever the occasion, including recognition of successful collaboration.

### Case study:   Special awards encourage collaboration

Participants in many cross-organizational collaborative ventures have devised mechanisms to recognize when individuals or organizations are doing things right. Benefits are three-fold:

◆ Participants appreciate genuine recognition for the collaborative efforts.

◆ All participants become more conscious of effective collaborative behavior and potentially improve their own through improved knowledge.

◆ Focusing on successful collaborative efforts sets a tone of trust and respect, and builds up the collaborative relationship.

Following good practice for rewarding people, examples include:

◆ Giraffe awards – used by one collaborative venture to recognize individuals who 'stick their necks out' to help others independent of job descriptions, time zones or organizational boundaries.

◆ Bouquets – special note cards used by participants in one collaborative venture to say 'thank you' to colleagues.

◆ News notes – vignettes published on a rotating basis where one constituency described the successful collaborative efforts of another.

◆ Team bonus – aligning compensation to reflect degree to which all are satisfied with genuine collaboration._____

## Key Tools and Techniques

Do not assume that the collaborative efforts you have begun will continue to serve you well if they are left unattended. As the laws of physics proclaim, 'Left to themselves, things tend to get worse.' To sustain successful collaboration across organizational boundaries:

✔ Ensure that collaboration is everyone's responsibility by incorporating, for every participant, specific goals and objectives with respect to collaborative behaviors.

✔ Follow up and follow through on the agreements reached in the initial phase of your partnering relationship – particularly agreements about how you and your colleagues will work together, who is doing what to whom, in what way, with what expected result.

✔ Submit your collaborative venture to a periodic checkup where you assess and improve how well you and your colleagues are doing with respect to:
  – alignment of purpose
  – ability to perform
  – attention to process
  – acuity of communication
  – attitude of trust and respect
  – adaptability to learn and change.

✔ Test and enrich your recovery mechanism to be certain that it is strong enough to handle likely mistakes of individual situations throughout the life of your venture.

✔ Know when it is time to take corrective action.

✔ Explicitly acknowledge and reward your success in order to nurture the collaborative spirit of your venture, and to encourage you and your colleagues to continue to grow and invest in your relationship.

*As the leaders go,*
*so goes the*
*collaboration.*

CHAPTER 10

# The Role of the Leader(s)

R egardless of your seniority, title, authority or role, and whatever your sphere of influence in a business partnering venture, if you have and use the ability to influence your colleagues, then you are a leader. As the leaders go, so goes the enterprise. As a result, you have an extra responsibility in ensuring successful collaboration across organizational boundaries.

As a leader you must be engaged in the collaborative process – actively, visibly and continuously. The role you play and the behaviors you demonstrate can build up or tear down collaboration.

> For collaboration to flourish, your behavior must be collaborative.

Like many of your colleagues, perhaps you have achieved a leadership position based on your technical expertise, your years of experience and/or your problem-solving ability. It is imperative that you know that your accountability now as a leader is more than that of accomplishing the task at hand. You also influence and impact the success of collaboration based on whether and how:

- All involved in your venture remain in sync with the vision.
- Others are being developed, supported, encouraged and guided.
- Your collaborative venture remains alive, learning, growing and changing throughout its lifetime.
- You behave as a role model for the desired collaborative behaviors.

## Balancing Task and Relationship

To build successful collaboration across organizational boundaries you must balance the 'what' and the 'how' of your job so that each task gets done well and positive relationships with your colleagues are preserved. As one executive puts it: 'We want the bottom line result to be good and the journey to be pleasant, too.'

As shown in Figure 20, your ability to focus on tasks is in some ways orthogonal to your ability to focus on relationships. Yet you must do both.

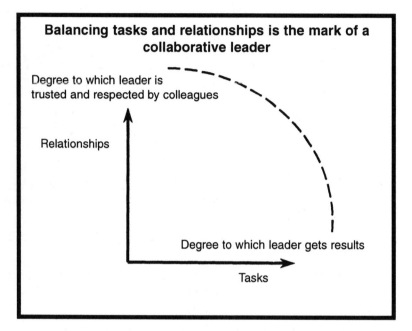

Fig. 20.   Balancing tasks and relationships as a leader.

Moment by moment you have to be able to determine when and how to:

- ◆ Charge ahead, moving everyone else out of your way if necessary, to get the job done.
- ◆ Back off entirely, letting your colleagues take center stage.
- ◆ Accommodate the needs and desires of your colleagues, even if you disagree.
- ◆ Negotiate with your colleagues to affect a workable compromise, finding enough common ground to move forward.
- ◆ Co-develop a creative solution with your colleagues, incorporating thoughts and ideas from everyone involved.

> To ensure successful collaboration across organizational boundaries how you go about your work is equally important as what you do.

There is an annual foot race run in San Francisco, California, named Bay to Breakers. Entrants run from a starting line by the Bay to the finish line by the ocean 'breakers', approximately seven miles, up and down hills. Those in the front of the pack can actually finish the race, all seven miles, before some in the back of the pack have set down their coffee cups and put on their numbers.

The same is true in collaborative ventures in a business setting. You as a leader may have a clear vision regarding desired outcome, beam yourself forward to the desired future, and mentally and emotionally finish the race before your colleagues have begun. Or you may concentrate only on your personal task(s), and not on the success of all collectively.

If you are to be an effective leader in a collaborative venture, you will ensure that:

- ♦ Your vision of the desired outcome is large enough to include both 'what' is to be accomplished and 'how' both you and your colleagues are to be involved.
- ♦ Your colleagues have the same vision of success as you do.
- ♦ All understand and are competent to perform their roles in the venture.
- ♦ Your personal deliverables align and integrate with those of your colleagues.
- ♦ Efforts of all are coordinated.
- ♦ All participants are encouraged and supported appropriately.
- ♦ Obstacles are removed along the way.

**Case study: Alliance agreements balance tasks and relationships**_____

One emerging company concentrated its expertise on selling and servicing customers. The leaders of the company decided, as part of the company's strategy, not to hire employees to build an internal capability to deliver education and training services to its customers. Instead, the firm forms alliances with key organizations and individuals in the industry who are experts in their fields.

The success of this collaborative business venture has been determined in part by shared values, the 'governing ideals – what we express and what we live'. For this venture these values include:

- integrity
- communication
- business effectiveness
- diversity
- trust
- accountability
- personal satisfaction
- team orientation.

Leaders in all the organizations involved are counted on to both accomplish tasks and preserve relationships. The values are reviewed periodically, and day-to-day management of performance throughout the collaboration is based on working together in accordance with these values. _____

## Getting Results

Make no mistake; effective leaders in collaborative ventures get results. You must ensure that you and your colleagues make progress toward your task objectives. The challenge is to do this without breaking relationships, or conversely, while building or maintaining healthy relationships with those involved in your venture. To get bottom line business results while you and your colleagues enjoy the experience of working together, you must:

- Be clear on the purpose of your venture, and how success will be measured both in terms of task and relationship.
- Ensure that all involved are:
  - competent to perform the work at hand
  - committed to doing whatever it takes to get the job done
  - courageous enough to make things happen.
- Follow through to monitor and manage performance on an ongoing basis.

Without real business results your collaborative venture will evolve to a social engagement or fall apart.

**Case study:   Cross-organizational team improves product reliability_____**
New situations may call for new and different ways of doing things. For example, in one alliance across two high tech companies, fundamental responsibilities were split as follows:

- Company A had primary responsibility for marketing, sales, customer service and product design.

♦ Company B had primary responsibility for product development and manufacturing.

Primary responsibility for product reliability belonged to Company B as part of the product development and manufacturing process. Yet, when faced with serious product reliability problems in the marketplace, leaders in this collaborative venture assembled a cross-organizational team of key representatives from both companies. The purpose of this team was two-fold:

♦ Address current product reliability problems in the field.
♦ Improve reliability characteristics of future products.

The team was not restricted by earlier established roles and responsibilities. Working together, the team:

♦ Investigated causes of the product failures.
♦ Developed short-term solutions to resolve the product reliability problems.
♦ Worked with customers and alliance representatives in the field to restore confidence and trust.
♦ Coordinated and cooperated with existing organizational entities.
♦ Recommended design changes for future products.
♦ Prepared the business plan for moving forward.

By breaking through existing organizational barriers and managing fuzzy boundaries this alliance proved successful in turning around a bad situation and positioning itself for long-term success. _____

## Creating Leverage

> To be an effective leader in a collaborative venture you must make your colleagues' strengths effective and their weaknesses irrelevant.

To do the above means that you must know your colleagues' strengths and weaknesses, both as individuals and organizations. You must know when and how to trust them thoroughly to accomplish things on their own, and when to follow up or support them in some way. To miss the mark on this means that you run the risk of:

♦ undermining their trust and respect
♦ invoking unnecessary checks and balances
♦ incurring unnecessary costs.

Get to know your colleagues. The more you understand and appreciate them, the more influence you can have as a leader.

**Case study:   Self-assessment helps improve collaboration** _____

In one collaborative venture involving 25 senior professionals from around the world, participants were invited to 'take inventory' of their strengths and weaknesses as related to their specific venture. The purpose of the exercise was to:

- ◆ Test for alignment and buy-in with respect to the overall objectives of the venture.
- ◆ Build honesty and candor among participants by testing self-disclosure.
- ◆ Determine whether the strengths of these 25 people would be sufficient for the venture.

The inventory took place in two phases. First, participants completed a survey like the one in Figure 21. Responses were consolidated, summarized and presented back to the team for review. Then, during a facilitated work session, each participant presented a personalized promise and request to the group in the following format:

Throughout the life of this venture

1   You can count on me to . . .
2   I will need your support and/or help with . . .
3   I am committed to improve on my ability to . . .

The results?

- ◆ Two more people were added to the team to round out skills.
- ◆ Trust and confidence among participants grew as they experienced each other living up to the promises made.
- ◆ Collaboration grew based on specific requests the participants made of each other._____

---

## Strengths/Weaknesses Self-Assessment

*With respect to this venture, I bring the following:*

1 Personal strengths
2 Personal weaknesses
3 Priority for personal development

Fig. 21.   Strengths / weaknesses self-assessment.

## Facilitating the Process

Your role as a leader in a collaborative venture is a lot like the role of a lubricant in mechanical equipment. You must keep all parts working. You must fill voids, ease frictions and tension, and enable others to contribute their best. Over and above just getting your own work done, you will find yourself:

◆ Reconciling frames of reference among individuals and across organizations.
◆ Resolving task-related and relationship-related conflicts.
◆ Coaching and mentoring your colleagues with respect to both content and process.
◆ Checking for alignment about purpose and priorities.
◆ Communicating a lot with your colleagues.
◆ Ensuring that everyone participates appropriately.

As one executive puts it, 'A leader in a cross-organizational collaboration is a manager of other people's commitments, an enabler for communication, and a catalyst to unstick stuck stuff.'

**Case study:  Leader ensures that everyone contributes to shared vision __**
To develop a shared vision for their collaborative venture, Melody enlisted the help of key representatives from the six organizations involved. She guided them through the following process:

◆ Document individual expectations for this venture – what each organization envisions as success.
◆ Present their lists so that everyone's perspective is heard and understood by all.
◆ Identify those points of agreement on which to build their collaboration.
◆ Reconcile discrepancies and disagreements regarding what to do and how to proceed.
◆ Clarify priorities to focus participants' energies on what they can achieve together.
◆ Develop individual objectives and performance plans to support the desired outcome._____

## Practicing What You Preach

At the beginning of each airline flight, as part of the safety briefing, we are all reminded that in the event that oxygen masks are needed, we should put on our own masks before attempting to assist someone else. The same idea holds in creating successful collaboration across organizational boundaries. Before you can expect others to collaborate with you, you must collaborate with them. Get your behavior straight before you can expect others to do so.

Assess your own collaborative behavior. Be honest. For example:

- How well do you understand and identify with the vision and/or purpose for your venture (Chapter 2)?
- How clear are your values, and how well do they align with those of the rest of the group?
- How passionate are you about the objectives of your venture?
- How well do you understand your role, responsibility and accountability with respect to the venture?
- How competent are you in terms of function, form and fit (Chapter 3) to perform in your assigned role?
- How compliant are you with regard to the policies, procedures, processes (Chapter 4) that exist for your venture?
- How well do you keep your colleagues informed and involved?
- How effective and efficient is your communication (Chapter 5) with others?
- How generously do you listen to your colleagues?
- How much do you trust and respect (Chapter 6) your colleagues?
- How much do you practice common courtesy with your colleagues?
- How well do you understand and genuinely value your colleagues' frames of reference?
- How well do you show your personal appreciation for your colleagues' contributions?
- How effectively do you learn from your experiences (Chapter 7) and incorporate your learning into new situations?

Looking again at the list above, which of these do you do particularly well which is your weakest area? What makes it so? What overall grade would you give yourself for collaboration?

Now for the hard question. If your colleagues were to answer these questions about you, what would they say? What grade would your colleagues give you?

Finally, regardless of the grade that you would give yourself or that your colleagues would give you, in what area can you improve today?

As a leader you have a responsibility to practice what you preach. If collaboration is to be successful let it start with you, with your personal contribution to ensure:

- alignment of purpose
- ability to perform
- attention to process
- acuity of communication
- attitude of trust and respect
- adaptability to learn and change.

You should be a role model for successful collaborative behavior, 24 hours a day, seven days a week.

## Case study: One vote per person

In one alliance, professional services practitioners convene twice a year to pay out bonuses from the pool of income. Wishing to share bonuses based on performance they established the following mechanism:

- Each person presents a short summary of his/her contributions since the last meeting.
- Others discuss and add to the summaries as appropriate.
- Using a worksheet such as the one shown in Figure 22, each person apportions a total of 100 points among all individuals including themselves, according to the agreed achievements, qualities, and characteristics.
- Points from all the individual worksheets are added together and consolidated into one for review by the group.
- Bonuses are given based on each individual's overall score.
- Plans are agreed for individual growth and development.

By using this mechanism to monitor, reward and manage performance, collaboration is at work:

- Each member of the alliance is accountable to the whole group.
- Each member provides feedback to others.
- Everything is done 'in public'.
- Each member of the alliance knows where he/she stands relative to the whole.
- Leadership for this venture is shared.

| Performance Bonus Worksheet | | | | | |
|---|---|---|---|---|---|
| | **John** | **Matthew** | **Susan** | **Tom** | **Total** |
| *Customer satisfaction* | 20 | 12 | 20 | 8 | 60 |
| *Revenue and profit contribution* | 12 | 8 | 8 | 24 | 52 |
| *Leadership* | 12 | 4 | 24 | 12 | 52 |
| *Quality of work* | 32 | 24 | 24 | 16 | 96 |
| *Teamwork and collaboration* | 32 | 20 | 24 | 8 | 84 |
| *Integrity, trust and respect* | 20 | 16 | 16 | 4 | 56 |
| *Total score* | 128 | 84 | 116 | 72 | 400 |

Fig. 22.   Sample performance bonus worksheet.

# Enhancing Your Personal Effectiveness as a Leader

Recall the model for Situational Leadership promoted by Kenneth Blanchard, Ph.D. This model identifies four different leadership styles – directing, coaching, supporting and delegating – derived from two basic leadership behaviors – supportive and directive. Dr. Blanchard encourages leaders to use the four leadership styles situationally, depending on the development levels of those being led.

Building on the Situational Leadership model, all your interactions with others require some amount of task-focused behavior and some amount of relationship-focused behavior:

*Task-focused behavior*
- **Telling** others what to do, how, where and when to do it
- **Making decisions** about what and how things are to be done
- **Supervising** performance.

*Relationship-focused behavior*
- **Listening** to others
- **Asking** questions to draw out others' input
- **Encouraging** others
- **Facilitating** others' involvement in problem-solving and decision-making.

How would you describe your usual personal behavior as a leader? Consider whether you prefer to:

- **Instill** your thoughts and ideas into others by structuring their work, making decisions and directing their actions.
- **Instruct** others by teaching and coaching them, watching them perform and providing constructive feedback to help them grow and develop.
- **Inspire** others by praising, encouraging and motivating them to do their best.
- **In-trust** to others by delegating work and turning over day-to-day decision-making.

You may say that you use all types of leadership behavior equally well. If so, excellent, that is the intention. However, be careful; it is important that you distinguish:

- Instilling or instructing others versus doing the work yourself.
- In-trusting accountability, authority, and responsibility to others versus abdicating your responsibility to stay informed and involved.
- Inspiring your colleagues versus smothering them or leaving them alone all together.
- Which behavior(s) you think you are using versus the behavior(s) that your colleagues actually experience from you, especially when you are stressed or feeling pressure.

If you answer that you don't know which is your usual behavior, the first order of business for you is to look at your behavior to see what you are doing.

Looking a little more closely at these choices, you will see that each comprises some amount of desire on your part to build relationships along with some desire to complete the task at hand:

- Instructing and inspiring require that you invest in building relationships with your colleagues, meeting them where they are.
- Instilling requires that you focus more on getting the task done.
- In-trusting demands that you have trust and confidence in your colleagues' abilities to perform the task at hand and in the relationship between you.

To be effective as a leader, you need to be conscious of your behavior, and it must be purposeful in each situation.

> Your behavior needs to be appropriate for the individuals and organizations you want to lead.

In particular, in collaborative ventures your behavior needs to be appropriate for the other individual's or organization's competence, commitment and courage – in the specific situation:

- Competence – including function (technical knowledge related to the work to be done within your venture), form (skill to do the job in the manner that you want/need it to be done), and fit (how the other person's or organization's knowledge and skills work compatibly with those of others involved in your venture).
- Commitment – to your venture and its success, the task to be done, you as an individual and a leader.
- Courage – the measure of motivation the other person or organization has to do what needs to be done (some call this WIIFM – what's in it for me).

As described in Chapter 8, the other person's or organization's competence, commitment and courage are interrelated, and they fluctuate. Typically:

- Competence goes up as task complexity goes down; and down as the task gets more complex.
- Commitment goes up based on your confidence in the person; and down as you show signs of distrust.
- Courage goes up as the level of risk goes down; and down as risk increases

For tasks where a colleague expresses confidence based on the fact that he/she is familiar with the issues and his/her competence is high, you should behave differently from if that same colleague has never performed the task before and appears tentative.

Your challenge is to understand where each of your colleagues is with respect to what you are trying to accomplish and choose your behavior accordingly. To assist you in matching your behavior to the specific situation, review the table in Figure 23.

| Effective leadership behavior | Follower's: | | |
|---|---|---|---|
| | Competence | Courage | Commitment |
| *Instruct* | Low | Low | Low |
| *Instill* | Low | Low | High |
| *Instruct* | Low | High | Low |
| *Instill* | Low | High | High |
| *Inspire* | High | Low | Low |
| *In-trust* | High | High | High |
| *Inspire* | High | High | Low |
| *Inspire* | High | Low | High |

Fig. 23.  Effective leadership behavior.

Regardless of your title, years of experience or amount of gray hair, if you are working with competent colleagues who are committed to your venture and motivated to do the right things, there is little need for task-focused directive leadership behavior on your part. Rather, you should expect to spend a lot of your leadership energy listening to your colleagues, drawing them out, and facilitating or participating in dialogue to co-develop appropriate solutions and action plans for moving forward. Conversely, if your colleagues are new to the work, or do not know much about how things need to be done in your venture, you should expect to coach them and provide encouragement rather than leaving them to their own devices.

Also, remember that as much as 98 per cent of the essence of leadership in a collaborative venture is the choice and practice of communicating with and influencing others. This means that you must choose to instill, instruct, inspire or in-trust your colleagues in a way that genuinely connects with them. For example:

♦ Where you are in-trusting accountability to your colleagues, make sure that you check up front for alignment to ensure that you have the same expectations about what is supposed to be done. Additionally, schedule and conduct progress checkpoint(s) along the way.

◆ Allow for the fact that, day by day, situation by situation, your colleagues' competence, commitment and/or courage may not be as high as you need them to be. When this is so, spend a little more time clarifying your expectations and getting the other person's buy-in to move forward.

◆ When you are coaching or instructing others:
  – explain the purpose and importance of what you want them to accomplish and why
  – define the process to be used to achieve results
  – show the person how to do the job
  – observe while the person practices
  – provide immediate and specific feedback regarding both what you like and what needs to be improved
  – express confidence in the person's ability to succeed
  – agree on next steps and follow up.

◆ To inspire your colleagues:
  – check for alignment and buy-in regarding key result areas and expectations
  – get their input in advance regarding anything that impacts them
  – ensure that they have adequate resources and appropriate tools to do the job
  – listen generously to their input, ideas, issues and concerns
  – provide praise and recognition – even your personal thanks makes a difference
  – trust them to do the right job in the right way.

◆ Enrich your technique in dealing with others so that in all of your interactions with others you can be genuine. Even if you have concerns or need to criticize a colleague's work, make a conscious choice to do so in a way that deals with the situation, yet builds up the other person.

◆ Find the appropriate balance between your desire to control your colleagues and their need to have freedom. As shown in Figure 24, for collaboration to be successful you must find the 'sweet spot' unique to your venture where you as a leader have an appropriate amount of control and your colleague(s) as follower(s), an appropriate amount of freedom.

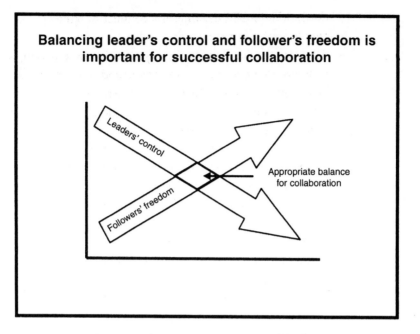

**Balancing leader's control and follower's freedom is important for successful collaboration**

Leaders' control

Followers' freedom

Appropriate balance
for collaboration

Fig. 24.   Balance between control and freedom.

### Case study:   Vice president engages a coach to enhance his personal effectiveness _____

Mike, a vice president in a Silicon Valley firm, was faced with having to lead a number of cross-organizational collaborative efforts as his company pursued many alliances with outside firms. To maximize both his business success and personal satisfaction, he engaged an executive coach to help him strengthen his leadership skills.

During a series of coaching sessions, Mike was able to build on his personal strengths and overcome weaknesses in his leadership style. In particular, he learned to:

◆ Treat all individuals and organizations with genuine respect, the same way he treats customers.
◆ Minimize any cause for disappointment in his colleagues by:
  - Checking for alignment before delegating to others, and conducting progress checkpoint meetings along the way.
  - Clarifying his own expectations and coaching colleagues more in specific situations where their competence, commitment or courage are not as high as he wants them to be.
  - Transforming his attitude to accept that others might not perform perfectly in all situations.

♦ Spend his time on those issues and opportunities of most importance to the venture.

By improving his own behavior Mike was able to be a more effective leader in many different collaborative efforts across organizational boundaries. _____

## Key Tools and Techniques

Regardless of your position, as you influence others you are a leader. To be effective:

✔ Know yourself – your strengths, weaknesses and preferred leadership style.

✔ Know your colleagues – their strengths, weaknesses and preferred behavioral styles so that you can make their strengths effective and their weaknesses irrelevant in your venture.

✔ Enhance your personal leadership behavior to include the full range of instilling, instructing, inspiring and trusting others, so that you can lead your colleagues from where they are.

✔ Be a role model for collaborative behaviors – 24 hours a day, seven days a week.

✔ Ensure that in all of your interactions with others you are building up, not tearing down.

✔ Facilitate the process so that all contribute appropriately.

✔ For your venture find appropriate balances between:
  – tasks and relationships
  – results and efforts
  – control and freedom.

CHAPTER 11

# Your Personal Action Plan

G iven that you made it to this point in the book, you must have a desire to build or improve a real collaborative business relationship. Remind yourself of your objective - for example:

- ◆ Enable a corporate merger or acquisition.
- ◆ Create a joint venture or strategic alliance.
- ◆ Manage multiple companies or organizations for a fast-track development project.
- ◆ Outsource a function or service.
- ◆ Create a sustaining business relationship with a key vendor or supplier.
- ◆ Energize a faltering collaborative venture.
- ◆ Become a better team mate.

So what will you do next? For example, you could:

- ◆ Pretend that you did not read this book and go about your business in the same way as before.
- ◆ Confirm with your colleagues that all is well with your collaborative venture and encourage the group to carry on.
- ◆ Determine that your collaborative venture needs help – that something(s) need to be stopped, started or changed in order for collaboration to be successful.
- ◆ Believe that you are doing things very well, but that your colleagues need to collaborate better.
- ◆ Understand that you need to improve your own interpersonal behavior.
- ◆ Want to do all of the above.

Or, you could make a difference. As one executive says when faced with what to do next: 'If it is to be, it's up to me.'

## Conducting a Self-Assessment

Conduct an honest assessment of your personal behavior. Reflect on your recent experiences working with your colleagues. What went well, and what would you do differently if given the opportunity? How do others respond to you?

Look at all aspects of your work – both what you accomplish and how you go about doing your job. Remember that to build successful collaboration across organizational boundaries you must balance the 'what' and the 'how' of your job so that you:

- Perform each task well – others can count on you to deliver on your commitments.
- Develop and maintain positive relationships with your colleagues – both the individuals and the organizations involved in your venture.

Ask yourself how well you:

- Deliver results and follow through according to your agreed responsibilities and commitments to your colleagues.
- Behave as a team player, supporting the team's decisions as your own.
- Communicate effectively and efficiently with others.
- Use your manners and common courtesy in dealing with others.
- Engender trust and respect among your colleagues.
- Adhere to agreed processes and systems for getting things done in your venture.
- Make your commitments known to others.
- Achieve closure as necessary.
- Include others as appropriate for decision-making, problem resolution, etc.
- Share information freely and on a timely basis.
- Balance being proactive and reactive in your work.
- Solicit and incorporate feedback from your colleagues as a regular part of your work.
- Value and appreciate your colleagues.
- Understand and buy-in to the overall vision and goals of the group.
- Serve as an effective role model for others regarding collaboration.

To assist you with this exercise, refer to the Interpersonal Behavior Assessment Worksheet in Appendix B of this book. If you wish to conduct your personal assessment in conjunction with an assessment of your collaborative group as a whole, refer to the Group Dynamics Assessment Worksheet in Appendix C.

The objective of your self-assessment is to help you:

◆ Identify and build on your personal strengths.
◆ Overcome and/or minimize the impact of your weaknesses.
◆ Behave as a role model for the desired collaborative behaviors.

**Case study: Self-assessment is input for performance reviews** _____

In one worldwide venture, participants take time on an annual basis to conduct self-assessments. Each participant's self-assessment is used in conjunction with evaluations from peers to form the basis for their performance reviews and distribution of bonus pay.

Each member of the team rates himself / herself against the combination of accomplishments and attributes shown in Figure 25. _____

## Expanding Your Personal Operating Behavior

For collaboration to flourish you must collaborate. That means that you must perform your work in relationship with your colleagues. As previously stated, to ensure successful collaboration across organizational boundaries how you go about your work is as important as what you do.

### Personal preference for task and relationship

Using Figure 26 as a guide, consider your personal preferences for task and relationship in your work. Mentally plot yourself somewhere on the chart according to your usual mode of operation, when things are going well and you are left to your own devices. Mark that spot in your mind with an 'N'.

Look again at the chart and mentally plot your mode of operation when you are under pressure or feeling stressed. Mark that spot in your mind with an 'S'. Notice whether and how your mode of operation changes as your circumstances change.

Then connect the 'N' and the 'S' with a line or box to define your preferred 'operating behavior'. The line or box may be large or small, and it may move up, down or sideways.

| Team member evaluation criteria | |
|---|---|
| *Results orientation* | ◆ Meets agreed objectives and commitments to others.<br>◆ Manages customer expectations and achieves customer satisfaction.<br>◆ Makes things happen.<br>◆ Makes no excuses.<br>◆ Develops options and prioritizes real time. |
| *Financial management and resource utilization* | ◆ Ensures that the company receives value for cost.<br>◆ Understands and manages/influences budget in relation to other functions.<br>◆ Identifies and manages cost variations early.<br>◆ Leverages and balances resources to maximize productivity. |
| *Development of self and staff* | ◆ Develops self, staff and others through proactive coaching and training.<br>◆ Ensures that this group learns from projects and ongoing activities.<br>◆ Maintains an accurate assessment of self and others – knows how to play to personal strengths and minimize the impact of weaknesses. |
| *Leadership* | ◆ Is able to collaborate and influence internally and externally at all organizational levels.<br>◆ Serves as an effective role model for others.<br>◆ Builds and leads cross-functional teams and non-traditional work groups.<br>◆ Leads others effectively whether as a direct line report or as a colleague.<br>◆ Works effectively on a global basis, with respect for different cultures and customs.<br>◆ Resolves conflict effectively, and in a timely manner.<br>◆ Personally exhibits and instills in others timely and responsive customer service skills.<br>◆ Manages through ambiguity.<br>◆ Demonstrates optimism, enthusiasm and high energy that translate into positive action. |
| *Business judgment* | ◆ Maintains appropriate business context for his/her work.<br>◆ Thinks globally – maintains a holistic view.<br>◆ Can be trusted to act on behalf of and in concert with all aspects of the venture.<br>◆ Demonstrates high integrity – does the right thing. |
| *Teamwork* | ◆ Is effective as both a team leader as well as a team member.<br>◆ Has gained the respect and trust of others at all levels.<br>◆ Shows respect for others.<br>◆ Supports other team members' goals. |
| *Effective communication* | ◆ Provides timely and appropriate verbal and written communication with all involved.<br>◆ Listens generously to others.<br>◆ Keeps self informed. |

Fig. 25.   Sample team member evaluation criteria.

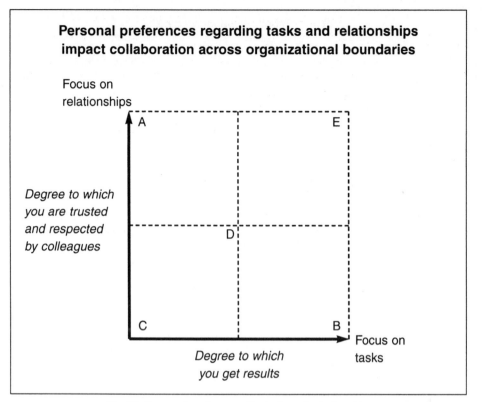

**Personal preferences regarding tasks and relationships impact collaboration across organizational boundaries**

Focus on relationships

A

E

*Degree to which you are trusted and respected by colleagues*

D

C

B

Focus on tasks

*Degree to which you get results*

Fig. 26. Personal preferences for task and relationship.

Remember that all points on the chart – all personal preferences for task and relationship – are appropriate, *depending on the situation* (as described in Chapter 3):

♦ Point A represents a strong preference on your part for relationship with your colleagues. You will probably accommodate the needs of your colleagues at your own expense, potentially focusing on the relationship at the risk of not getting any tasks accomplished. To extreme, you might become so accommodating of others that you add no unique value of your own.

♦ Point B represents a strong preference on your part to accomplish tasks. You are likely to concentrate on getting the job done at the expense of relationship with your colleagues. This may appear expedient in the short run, but taken to extremes you might become so focused that you work without any regard at all for the collaborative efforts of the group.

♦ Point C represents a preference for withdrawing from the

venture. You are not likely to have much impact on tasks or relationships if this is your position. Appropriate in some circumstance, you are what some would call a 'non-player'.

◆ Point D represents a preference for finding the middle ground with your colleagues, accomplishing some amount of task work while enjoying some relationship with them. You are likely to seek approval or compromise before proceeding with the work at hand.

◆ Point E represents a preference for putting in the time and energy required to work actively with others while getting the job done – to accomplish results while remaining in relationship with your colleagues. You are likely to spend much more time in communication with others than you would if you were just working on tasks by yourself, and you are likely to gain significant input from others to help you get your job done. To extreme, it can take a long time to get anything done.

Take care to grow your preferred operating behavior to include the full range of behavior choices so that your behavior can be appropriate for the business situation. For example:

◆ In an emergency you may need to gravitate toward point B, taking charge to get yourself and others out of harm's way.

◆ If consensus is building among your colleagues around a particular plan of action with which you disagree, you may have to move toward point A. You may need to commit to moving forward with the group even if you disagree.

◆ In those circumstances where a creative multi-faceted solution is needed you may need to gravitate toward point E, willing, ready and able to spend whatever time and energy is required to work actively with your colleagues to generate the right solution.

### Personal preferences for control and belonging

In his interpersonal psychology work Dr Timothy Leary juxtaposed the individual's personal needs for control and belonging:

◆ Control – the degree to which you want to call the shots, to govern yourself and others, to be in charge; to dominate others.

- Belonging – the degree to which you desire to be part of the group, to affiliate with others.

Like children pulling at your sleeve, your personal needs for control and belonging impact your ability to collaborate with others.

By understanding and managing your needs for control and belonging you can expand the number of choices you have in working effectively across organizational boundaries.

Figure 27 offers a plot of these two:

- Your desire for control is represented vertically, with high at the top of the figure and low at the bottom.
- Your need for belonging is shown horizontally, with high to the right of the figure and low at the left.

Using Figure 27 as a guide, take a moment to locate where your needs fall. To what degree do you like to take charge (control)? And to what degree is it important to you to be part of the group (belonging)?

Look more closely at the following combinations of desire for control and belonging shown in Figure 27:

| *Quadrant* | *Control* | *Belonging* | *Characteristics* |
|---|---|---|---|
| *1* | *High* | *Low* | *Pathfinders – self-reliant and self-respecting; typically frank and honest, and able to be strict with self and others; like to set and act on their own priorities.* |
| *2* | *High* | *High* | *Cooperative leaders – considerate of others and helpful; typically well thought of by others and able to give orders; happy to lead others in a collaborative setting.* |
| *3* | *Low* | *Low* | *Problem-finders – able to doubt and criticize; typically skeptical, yet can be obedient if confident in direction good at identifying potential problems.* |

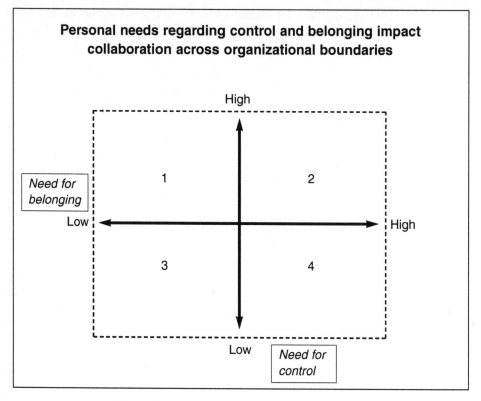

Fig. 27.   Personal needs for control and belonging.

| 4 | Low | Low | Team players – friendly and cooperative; typically appreciative of others' efforts and results; have little desire to take charge. |

All four combinations describe possible collaborators. All combinations also describe possible organizational models. By design or by accident, entire organizations can be either or both:

- driven to control
- motivated to belong to a larger enterprise.

You need to be able to recognize and deal with your own needs and desires, and those of your colleagues. You must be able to choose and use appropriate behaviors.

   Note that for both your personal preference for task and relationships, and your level of desire for control and belonging, 'low' and 'high' are relative terms. What may seem high to you could be considered low by your colleagues depending on their definitions and frames of reference. Hence, it is important for you to calibrate your self-knowledge with respect to the specific business context, and in relation to the organizations and individuals with whom you are working.

## *Matching Personal competence, commitment and courage with complexity, confidence and risk*

As described in Chapter 6, you present yourself to others based on the contents of your personal and professional calling card, your:

- professional expertise and accomplishments
- positional role and authority
- personal character and reputation.

These ingredients all work together to determine in each specific situation your levels of:

- competence
- commitment
- courage. (See Chapter 10.)

For collaboration to succeed your levels of competence, commitment and courage must match:

- the level of complexity of the task
- your colleagues' confidence in your ability to do the job
- the risk represented by the task.

So your challenge in all this is to ensure that your personal and professional calling card:

- is appropriate for your venture
- serves to build trust and confidence among your colleagues.

**Case study:  Professional service providers expand their operating behaviors**_____

A group of professional services partners found themselves criticized by others for not being collaborative. They were described as being:

- task driven
- uncaring about people
- mentally and emotionally abusive of others.

With input from all, they set out to become role models for collaborative behavior as follows:

- Perform well – discharge our tasks professionally and set task-related expectations with others.
- Communicate more with each other.
- Share information with others.
- Teach others.
- Delegate more, allowing others to grow.
- Include others, particularly peers and colleagues, in discussions and decision-making processes.
- Motivate others – 'bring people in'.
- Listen more.
- Understand how our own communication is being received.
- Treat others with courtesy – particularly civil communication.
- Reach closure more, not letting things hang.
- Give credit to others whenever possible – have a 'credit balance' with others.
- Balance our own lives.

Discussion revealed the need for all these partners to become more agile in dealing with others. For example, to be effective leaders of others, these partners need to be able to direct, delegate, coach and/or support others situationally. Each partner's choice of behavior should match both the other person's competence, commitment and courage with respect to the task at hand combined with:

- level of complexity of the task
- the leader's confidence in the person's abilities relative to the task
- the risk represented by the task.

In order to remain in relationship with their colleagues while getting their tasks accomplished, these partners had to become adept at utilizing a full range of personal behaviors. They identified the following priorities for improvement:

- Develop more patience with others.
- Proactively obtain feedback from others.
- Provide regular communication.
- Proactively resolve conflicts.
- Share information.
- Balance personal planning with action.
- Listen generously.
- 'Stroke' others – acknowledge their work and say 'thank you'.
- Spend more time teaching people._____

# Making the Right Choice

For collaboration to succeed you need to do your part. If you are ready, willing and able to do what it takes to collaborate with your colleagues in spite of whatever boundaries exist, you should be able to make a cogent statement, such as the one started for you in Figure 28, about your intended contribution to your collaborative venture.

---

### Personal Commitment to Collaboration

Throughout the life of this venture you can count on me to behave in the following ways based on my personal strengths:

I will need your assistance in the following way to help me overcome the following personal weaknesses:

I am committed to improve on my ability to collaborate in the following ways:

---

Fig. 28. Personal commitment to collaboration.

**Case study:  Joan and Peter must choose to collaborate** _____

Joan is an excellent marketing manager with an international company – brilliant, dynamic, high energy, very much appreciated by customers. She is an action-oriented negotiator who works quickly and cleverly. She is especially good at closing multi-million dollar transactions with customers, handling difficult customer situations, fire-fighting in the face of adversity and handling out of the ordinary or unexpected situations. She is business savvy and very creative. Joan works well with fellow marketing representatives and sales engineers around the world who are quick on their feet and situational in their approach to getting the job done. She also works well with senior engineers who create custom solutions in response to customers' requirements.

Joan struggles in working with Peter, the vice president of customer support. Peter has responsibility for post sales customer satisfaction. With customer support personnel around the world, Peter and his team care for the customers whom Joan and other marketing representatives bring in. He approaches his job in an organized manner, with a sense of duty, loyalty and industry. He adheres to policies and procedures and likes things to be done in an orderly fashion, by the book.

From Joan's perspective, Peter is often slow to respond, lacking any sense of urgency and seemingly unimpressed with the importance of dealing with Joan's customers. From Peter's perspective Joan is a rebel, always wanting special treatment, not wanting to play by the rules.

Yet they need each other in order to succeed. Without Peter's help to manage and grow the customer accounts once they exist, Joan's glory is short-lived. Likewise, without Joan's ability to close sales for the company, Peter and his subordinates will not have much to do.

To make this cross-organizational collaboration work, both Joan and Peter must learn and change. Both must:

♦ Expand their own parochial views of the world to also appreciate the value the other brings to the business.

♦ Choose to meet the needs of the other or take the time together to create a relationship that will work for them._____

## Using the Keys to Collaboration

You should include in your personal action plan some notes related specifically to the six keys to collaboration described in Part 1 of this book:

♦ alignment of purpose

♦ ability to perform

♦ attention to process

♦ acuity of communication

♦ attitude of trust and respect

♦ adaptability to learn and change.

Review the concepts and ideas presented, assess your status, and make it your business to collaborate with your colleagues. For example:

♦ Understand and buy-in to the vision and/or purpose for your venture.

♦ Clarify your values and ensure that they are aligned with those of the rest of the group.

♦ Confirm that the objectives for your venture evoke some amount of your passion.

♦ Understand your role, responsibility and accountability with respect to the venture.

♦ Make sure that you are competent in terms of function, form and fit, to perform in your assigned role.

◆ Comply with the policies, procedures, processes and guidelines that exist for your venture.
◆ Keep your colleagues informed and involved appropriately.
◆ Make your communication effective and efficient.
◆ Listen generously to your colleagues.
◆ Learn to trust and respect your colleagues.
◆ Practice common courtesy with your colleagues.
◆ Understand and genuinely value your colleagues' frames of reference.
◆ Show your personal appreciation for your colleagues' contributions.
◆ Learn from your experiences and incorporate your learning into new situations throughout the life of your venture.
◆ Serve as a role model for successful collaborative behavior, 24 hours a day, seven days a week.
◆ Identify, interaction by interaction, where each of your colleagues is with respect to what you are trying to accomplish and choose your behavior accordingly.

And, whatever your status is today, make a commitment to improve.

## Key Tools and Techniques

For collaboration to flourish, you must collaborate. In order to do your part:
✔ Know yourself – your strengths, weaknesses and preferred interpersonal behavior.
✔ Know your colleagues – their strengths, weaknesses, personalities and preferred behavioral styles so that you can interact with them where they are.
✔ Enhance your personal operating behavior to enable you to call on a wide range of behaviors to accomplish tasks and manage relationships.
✔ Ensure that in all of your interactions with others you are building up, not tearing down.
✔ Behave as a role model for collaborative behaviors – 24 hours a day, seven days a week.

# *Partnering in Action* Report Card

## Instructions

T he *Partnering in Action* Report Card provides a feedback mechanism for partnering relationships. Using the *Partnering in Action* framework the report card offers an easy way to build on what is working and to focus on those elements of the partnering relationship that need attention.

The *Partnering in Action* Report Card can be administered periodically in conjunction with a partnering work session.

## Prior to the Partnering Work Session

All participants should review the report card and:

1  In the column labeled Team Grade for this Period assign a grade (for example: A, B, C, D, F; or percentage scale of 0 to 100) for each of the six essential partnering elements. The grade is based on the individual Team Member's perception of how things are going.

2  In the column labeled Priority for Improvement check one or two of the six essential partnering elements on which the group should focus to improve the partnering relationship.

The facilitator / leader should collect the input from all team members and summarize it on one report card for discussion by the group.

## During the Partnering Work Session

1  The facilitator / leader should present a consolidation of all team members' responses to the *Partnering in Action* Report Card.

2  The group should discuss:
   • What these grades mean – for example: Are we partnering as we intended? Are we missing something?

- What is the most important area for the group to focus on now?

3 Based on the grades and priorities for improvement, the group should identify explicit next steps to improve the partnering relationship.

| *Partnering in Action* Report Card | | |
|---|---|---|
| *Essential partnering element* | *Team grade for this period* | *Priority for improvement* |
| Alignment of purpose – including shared business context; enterprise vision and mission; goals and objectives; priorities | | |
| Ability to perform – including getting the job done; contributing one's best; focusing on excellence; making a difference; individual and shared accountability for outcomes | | |
| Attention to process – including meeting management; management of tasks; progress monitoring and reporting; decision-making; problem solving; conflict resolution; governance; internal / external measurement systems | | |
| Acuity of communication – including openness / candor; discipline and skill to provide and receive information; fluidity of communication; timely and accurate feedback systems | | |
| Attitude of mutual trust and respect – including sharing risk / reward; blending autonomy and interdependence; spirit of acknowledgment and mutual support | | |
| Adaptability to learn and change – including after-action briefings; institutional memory; commitment to continuous improvement | | |
| Name (optional)_____ | Date_____ | |

# Interpersonal Behavior Assessment Worksheet

## Instructions

For each behavior characteristic listed below, circle in the column labeled Assessment the number that reflects how frequently members of this group demonstrate the behavior in their work:

| 1 | 2 | 3 | 4 | 5 |
|---|---|---|---|---|
| never | seldom | sometimes | often | always |

Finally, identify your personal best and worst characteristics as follows:

A.  In the column labeled B mark with an 'x' the two or three behavior characteristics which are your 'personal bests'.

B.  In the column labeled W mark with an 'x' the two or three behavior characteristics which are your 'personal worsts'.

| Behavior characteristic | Assessment 1 (never) – 5 (always) | B | W |
|---|---|---|---|
| 1  I hold myself accountable for results | 1  2  3  4  5 | | |
| 2  I keep my commitments to others | 1  2  3  4  5 | | |
| 3  I engage in regular communication with my colleagues through effective participation at meetings, concise and timely phone calls, and appropriate written correspondence | 1  2  3  4  5 | | |
| 4  I share information freely with my colleagues | 1  2  3  4  5 | | |
| 5  I include all stakeholders in the decision-making process | 1  2  3  4  5 | | |
| 6  I am an effective team player – I place the team's interests ahead of my own | 1  2  3  4  5 | | |

| 7 | I support and represent the team's decisions as my own | 1 2 3 4 5 | | | |
|---|---|---|---|---|---|
| 8 | I use good manners, common courtesy and tact when dealing with others involved in the collaborative venture | 1 2 3 4 5 | | | |
| 9 | I speak with honesty and candor | 1 2 3 4 5 | | | |
| 10 | I am patient with others, and slow to anger | 1 2 3 4 5 | | | |
| 11 | I listen generously to others, striving to understand others' points before seeking to be understood | 1 2 3 4 5 | | | |
| 12 | I show respect for all, regardless of gender, race, age, position | 1 2 3 4 5 | | | |
| 13 | I actively solicit and incorporate others' input, and do not insist on doing things my own way | 1 2 3 4 5 | | | |
| 14 | I acknowledge others' contributions by being quick to say thank you to others and give credit to others | 1 2 3 4 5 | | | |
| 15 | I find ways to build up others rather than criticize or tear them down | 1 2 3 4 5 | | | |
| 16 | I actively develop in others the knowledge and skills they need to achieve the venture's goals | 1 2 3 4 5 | | | |
| 17 | I am approachable and available as needed to answer questions, and to provide guidance and direction for others | 1 2 3 4 5 | | | |
| 18 | I resolve conflicts with ease by dealing with individuals directly, constructively, and confidentially | 1 2 3 4 5 | | | |
| 19 | I understand others' thoughts and feelings regarding how things are going because I proactively obtain feedback from them | 1 2 3 4 5 | | | |
| 20 | I am effective at balancing planning with action | 1 2 3 4 5 | | | |
| 21 | I know our customers – both external and internal – and focus on their needs | 1 2 3 4 5 | | | |

| | | | |
|---|---|---|---|
| 22  I ensure that closure is reached on decisions | 1  2  3  4  5 | | |
| 23  I delegate authority by encouraging decisions to be made at the appropriate level in the venture | 1  2  3  4  5 | | |
| 24  I serve as an effective role model for others regarding collaborative interpersonal behavior | 1  2  3  4  5 | | |

Appendix C

# Group Dynamics Assessment Worksheet

## Instructions

For each behavior characteristic listed below, circle in the column labeled Assessment the number that reflects how frequently members of this group demonstrate the behavior in their work:

| 1 | 2 | 3 | 4 | 5 |
|---|---|---|---|---|
| never | seldom | sometimes | often | always |

Then, for each of the behavior characteristics, in the column labeled Impact identify whether / how this behavior could improve performance for the organization as a whole – for example:

A. Increases productivity in this enterprise.
B. Contributes to reduced costs by reducing turnover, minimizing legal exposure, etc.
C. Offers personal growth for members of this group.

Finally, identify your personal best and worst characteristics as follows:

A. In the column labeled B mark with an 'x' the two or three behavior characteristics which are your 'personal bests'.
B. In the column labeled W mark with an 'x' the two or three behavior characteristics which are your 'personal worsts'.

| Behavior characteristic | Assessment 1 (never) – 5 (always) | Impact | B | W |
|---|---|---|---|---|
| 1   We hold ourselves and others accountable for results | 1   2   3   4   5 | | | |
| 2   We keep our commitments to others | 1   2   3   4   5 | | | |
| 3   We engage in regular communication with each other through effective participation at meetings, concise and timely phone calls, and appropriate written correspondence | 1   2   3   4   5 | | | |
| 4   We share information freely with each other, and with other managers, staff and employees | 1   2   3   4   5 | | | |
| 5   We include all stakeholders in the decision-making process | 1   2   3   4   5 | | | |
| 6   We are effective team players – we place the team's interests ahead of our own | 1   2   3   4   5 | | | |
| 7   We all support and represent the team's decisions as our own | 1   2   3   4   5 | | | |
| 8   We use good manners, common courtesy and tact when dealing with others in the venture | 1   2   3   4   5 | | | |
| 9   We speak with honesty and candor | 1   2   3   4   5 | | | |
| 10   We are patient with others and slow to anger | 1   2   3   4   5 | | | |
| 11   We listen generously to others, striving to understand others' points before seeking to be understood | 1   2   3   4   5 | | | |
| 12   We show respect for all, regardless of gender, race, age, position | 1   2   3   4   5 | | | |
| 13   We actively solicit and incorporate others' input and do not insist on doing things our own way | 1   2   3   4   5 | | | |
| 14   We acknowledge others' contributions by being quick to say thank you to others and give credit to others | 1   2   3   4   5 | | | |
| 15   We find ways to build up others rather than criticize or tear them down | 1   2   3   4   5 | | | |

| | | | | | |
|---|---|---|---|---|---|
| 16 | We actively develop in others the knowledge and skills they need to achieve the venture's goals | 1 2 3 4 5 | | | |
| 17 | We are approachable and available as needed to answer questions, and to provide guidance and direction for others | 1 2 3 4 5 | | | |
| 18 | We resolve conflicts with ease by dealing with individuals directly, constructively and confidentially | 1 2 3 4 5 | | | |
| 19 | We understand others' thoughts and feelings regarding how things are going because we proactively obtain feedback from them | 1 2 3 4 5 | | | |
| 20 | We are effective at balancing planning with action | 1 2 3 4 5 | | | |
| 21 | We know our customers – both external and internal – and focus on their needs | 1 2 3 4 5 | | | |
| 22 | We ensure that closure is reached on decisions | 1 2 3 4 5 | | | |
| 23 | We delegate authority by encouraging decisions to be made at the appropriate level in the organization | 1 2 3 4 5 | | | |
| 24 | We serve as effective role models for others regarding appropriate interpersonal behavior | 1 2 3 4 5 | | | |

# Cultural Alignment Worksheet
# Purpose, People and Practice

T his worksheet is for mergers, acquisitions, strategic alliances, joint ventures, sustaining business partnering relationships.

## Instructions

1  Working alone or with colleagues, review and note the qualities and characteristics related to each organization involved in your venture (use multiple worksheets as needed):
    –  purpose – the fundamental reason(s) the organizations exists
    –  people – care of and consideration for all involved
    –  practice – how the organizations operate.

2  Identify similarities and differences as follows:
    –  In the column labeled 'most' mark those items that are most aligned.
    –  In the column labeled 'least' mark those items that are most different.

3  Determine which items among those marked 'least' need your attention and develop a plan to create appropriate alignment.

| Qualities and characteristics of organizational culture | Organization A | Organization B | MOST | LEAST |
|---|---|---|---|---|
| *Alignment of purpose*<br>– Underlying philosophy – guiding principles, core values, 'stakes in the ground'<br><br>– Business value drivers – revenue growth, margin enhancement, capital efficiency and structure<br><br>– Business focus – customer focus versus product focus<br><br>– Business strategy – customers, markets, 'business promise', competitive positioning<br><br>– Measures of profitability and success – short-term versus long-term, objective versus subjective<br><br>– Other – | | | | |
| *Alignment of people*<br>– Core competencies – function, form, fit, experience, specialist versus generalist model, professional development, career path model<br><br>– Personnel policies – hire from outside versus promote from within, training / education, titles, job descriptions, ownership, performance versus seniority, managing expectations<br><br>– Organization structure – hierarchical versus flat, matrix or integrated, blend of staff and line functions, central versus distributed<br><br>– Compensation – types (salary, comp time, stock, bonus), cash versus stock philosophy and practice, pay scales, review period and process<br><br>– Benefits – types, policies and practices – medical, dental, vision, | | | | |

| | | | | |
|---|---|---|---|---|
| elder/child care, PTO, education, holiday, etc<br><br>– Code of conduct – personal behavior, dress, etc<br><br>– Facilities – open plan versus hard-wall plan, amenities, employee services<br><br>– Partners and suppliers – NIH versus alliances<br><br>– Other – | | | | |
| *Alignment of Practice*<br>– Decision-making – 'sign off' authority level, centralized versus decentralized, fast versus slow, proactive versus reactive, intuition versus analysis<br><br>– Accountability – individual versus shared, autonomy versus interdependence<br><br>– Information systems – number, types, in-house versus third party<br><br>– Key functions / processes – product development, marketing, sales, customer service, manufacturing, budgeting and financial management<br><br>– Communication tools and techniques – email versus voice mail, meetings – number and types, feedback systems<br><br>– Rewards and recognition – seniority versus achievement, individual versus team, cash versus stock, public versus private, recognition events<br><br>– Conflict / problem resolution – escalation procedure versus team construct, organized versus ad hoc, formal versus informal<br><br>– Other – | | | | |

Appendix E

# Additional Reading and Reference Material

*Alliance Advantage: The Art of Creating Value Through Partnering*, Yves L. Doz, Gary Hamel (Harvard Business School, 1998).

*Building Strategic Relationships: How to Extend Your Organization's Reach Through Partnerships, Alliances, and Joint Ventures*, Juli Betwee, David Meuel, William H. Bergquist, David Memel (Jossey-Bass Publishers, 1995).

*Business Alliances Guide: The Hidden Competitive Weapon*, Robert Porter Lynch (John Wiley & Sons, 1993).

*How Teamwork Works: The Dynamics of Effective Team Development*, John Syer, Christopher Connolly (McGraw-Hill, 1996).

*How to Make Meetings Work* Michael Doyle, David Straus (Jove Books, 1976).

*Intelligent Business Alliances: How to Profit Using Today's Most Important Strategic Tool*, Larraine Segil (Times Books, 1996).

*Leadership and the Art of Conversation*, Kim H. Krisco (Prima Publishing, 1997).

*Leadership and the One Minute Manager*, Kenneth Blanchard, Patricia Zigmari, Drea Zigmari, (Morrow and Co, 1985).

*Please Understand Me*, David Keirsey, Marilyn Bates (Prometheus Nemesis Book Co, 1984).

*Six Thinking Hats*, Edward de Bono (MICA Management Resources, Inc, 1985).

*Strategic Alliances: An Entrepreneurial Approach to Globalization*, Michael Y. Yoshino, U. Srinivasa Rangan, U. Srinivasa (Harvard Business School, 1995).

*Team Talk: The Power of Language in Team Dynamics*, Anne Donnellon (Harvard Business School, 1996).

*The Alliance Revolution: The New Shape of Business Rivalry*, Benjamin Bomes-Casseres (Harvard University, 1998).

*The Fifth Discipline Fieldbook*, Peter Senge, Art Kleiner, Charlotte Roberts, Richard Ross, Bryan Smith (Doubleday, 1994).

*The Team Building Tool Kit: Tips, Tactics and Rules for Effective Workplace Teams*, Deborah Harrington-MacKin (AMACOM, 1993).

*The Wisdom of Teams: Creating the High-Performance Organization*, Jon R. Katzenbach, Douglas K. Smith (Harperbusiness, 1994).

*Thinking Straight: A systematic guide to managerial problem-solving and decision-making that works*, Steve Kneeland (How To Books Ltd, 1999).

*Tips for Teams: A Ready Reference for Solving Common Team Problems*, Kimball Fisher, Steven Rayner, William Belgard (McGraw-Hill, 1994).

*Turning Team Performance Inside Out*, Susan Nash (How To Books Ltd, 2000).

*Why Teams Don't Work: What Went Wrong and How to Make It Right'* (audio cassette), Harvey Robbins, Michael Finley (HighBridge Company, 1997).

*Myers-Briggs Type Indicator®*, Katherine C. Briggs and Isabel Briggs Myers (Consulting Psychologists Press, Inc).

*Strength Deployment Inventory®*, Elias H. Porter (Personal Strengths Publishing, Inc).

# Index